REAL NEWS

AN INVESTIGATIVE REPORTER UNCOVERS THE FOUNDATIONS OF THE TRUMP-RUSSIA CONSPIRACY

SCOTT STEDMAN

Skyhorse Publishing, Inc.

Skyhorse Publishing books may be purchased in bulk at special discounts for sales promotion, corporate gifts, fund-raising, or educational purposes. Special editions can also be created to specifications. For details, contact the Special Sales Department, Skyhorse Publishing, 307 West 36th Street, 11th Floor, New York, NY 10018 or info@skyhorsepublishing.com.

Skyhorse® and Skyhorse Publishing® are registered trademarks of Skyhorse Publishing, Inc.®, a Delaware corporation.

Visit our website at www.skyhorsepublishing.com.

10 9 8 7 6 5 4 3 2 1

Library of Congress Cataloging-in-Publication Data is available on file.

ISBN: 978-1-5107-4678-7
eBook: 978-1-5107-4679-4

Cover design by Brian Peterson
Front cover photographs: AP Images

Printed in the United States of America

To Kirill Radchenko, Alexander Rastorguyev and Orkhan Dzhemal, your work exposing the dirty dealings of Vladimir Putin's Russia took you to the middle of Africa; your dedication to the truth took you to your graves.

Your pursuit of justice and integrity lives on in the young investigative journalists whom you inspired.

Table of Contents

Preface: Journalism that Combats Cries of Fake News 1

Introduction 13

Trump Tower Moscow and Dirty Russian Money 19

The Secret 2016 Manhattan Meetings 57

The Coffee Boy and His Mysterious Wife 87

Russian Infiltration of the National Rifle Association 117

Suspicious Business Dealings, Flights, and a Confession
    in Plain Sight 137

Epilogue 179

Who's Who: A Glossary of Key Trump-Russia Figures 183

Personal Acknowledgments 187

About the Author 188

Preface: Journalism that Combats Cries of Fake News

FACTS MATTER.

At a time in history in which those who hold the most powerful positions in the world seek to obfuscate by denying basic fact, it is imperative that the general public is overwhelmed with fact, truth, and empirical evidence.

The cries of "fake news!" cannot be allowed to go unchallenged.

The press is not the enemy of the people. The Fourth Estate is one of the shining indicators of the thriving democracy that America has loudly and proudly put on a pedestal for decades. It has exposed war crimes, detailed racism and injustice in the South, and brought down sitting presidents. There is nothing that good investigative journalism cannot do when it seeks to speak truth to power to hold it accountable, and doesn't stray from that mission.

In the era of journalists being body slammed, mocked, and ridiculed as fake news, we must return to the basics of journalism: Fact. Proof. Empirical evidence.

It is all too easy for those who dislike negative media coverage to attack the reporting itself when journalists fail to hold themselves to the highest standard possible. To combat these desperate cries of "fake news," journalists should not get offended, but rather return to the core of what a free press is supposed to do in this country and elsewhere: report the facts.

However, at the risk of sounding like an overzealous newcomer who's in over his head, I believe there must be fundamental changes in the way that investigative journalists go about their business. There is a growing segment of the population, especially among young adults, who finds themselves with a severe lack of trust in the news media. For those whose formative years were spent with the news coming largely from the internet and social media, there is a feeling of discouragement and apathy when it comes to politics and social issues. This discouragement is rooted in a lack of trust in any authoritative figure, in the media or elsewhere, to report facts without bias.

On TV, sex, drugs, drama, and violence are king. Major news channels largely fill their airtime with panels consisting of impassioned, partisan Democrats arguing with impassioned, partisan Republicans. Everyone involved in this setting is desperately seeking the ten-second "gotcha" sound clip that they can then share on Twitter in the hopes of feeding their crowdsourced hunger for affirmation. There's only one person in this scenario who is left entirely worse off: the American citizen.

The way that news is reported is broken. This feels taboo to say in light of some of the hate directed towards journalists at the behest of the most powerful people in the country, but there is a problem at the core of news reporting that needs to be addressed.

At the core of the problem lies a wave of opinion and speculation creeping into news reporting. A common tactic among those who consistently try to delegitimize the press is to conflate the editorial section of a publication with the news articles. Too often now, these sections are becoming increasingly difficult to distinguish.

From my perspective, I see three foundational changes that must be made by journalists to salvage the trust of the American people and fill the void left by figures from an earlier generation such as Walter Cronkite:

First, the hyperpartisanship in media for the sake of being entertaining has to be reined in.

Second, print journalists should return to the basics of

journalism by showing, not telling, and relying less on anonymous sources.

Finally, independent journalism must be recognized as an essential section of the media as a whole, so long as it doesn't devolve into conspiracy theories and wild speculation.

Me vs. You Media

What largely exists today is a "me vs. you" media that survives and thrives off of making those with whom you disagree into your enemies. Evening TV broadcasts on cable networks are the main purveyors of this ideology, as they profit when politics and news is transformed into entertainment.

I like to think of the normal blue-collar American worker who comes home from a hard day at work and turns on the news to see what has gone on in the world. What he or she finds on TV, however, is anything but the news. It's likely some Democrat yelling at a group of Republicans or vice-versa, with personal insults flying and a painful dearth of truth.

This attitude can also be widely found on social media, which has increasingly become infected with purposeful disinformation by foreign countries, bots, and trolls. These actors have no interest in sharing fact-based reporting, but rather feed off of the chaos and discord that comes from a hyperpartisan American population.

There is certainly a place for partisanship in the United States, though not in the world of investigative journalism. Disagreeing over politics and even slinging some mud is as American as apple pie. When there is no separation between these debates and fact-finding investigations, however, is when we as a population suffer the consequences.

In a similar vein, the "me vs. you" media is creating a dangerous echo chamber on both sides of the political spectrum. Studies have shown that people are becoming increasingly partisan and seeking out voices that affirm their political point of view. Social media is a culprit in this shift in approach from Americans, but not the only factor. Twitter, Facebook, Reddit and other platforms have certainly made it easier to "follow," "like," or "subscribe" to those who tell you what you want to hear. It's the path of least resistance. TV news profits by making politics as divided as possible, turning the discussion of political and social issues into a sport, putting profit over people.

In these uncertain and divisive times, a quote from the recent Dan Rather book, *What Unites Us*, rings all too prescient: "[A] democracy requires open access to ideas. It requires a willingness to struggle and learn, to question our own suppositions and biases, to open ourselves as citizens, and a nation, to a world of books and thought. If we become a country of superficiality and easy answers based on assumptions and not one steeped in reason and critical learning, we will have lost the foundation of our founding and all that has allowed our nation to grow into our modern United States."

It is more important now than ever for the press to recognize the commonality of the American citizen with his or her neighbor. The differences between us as Americans pale in comparison to those who wish to see actual harm to our democracy and institutions. Media that plays into the me vs. you narrative of extreme partisanship fulfills the wildest dreams of our true enemies around the world. There is nothing that Vladimir Putin, for instance, would want to see more than an America that became so hostile towards itself that it began to collapse from the inside.

"In recent years, Putin, his chief military strategist Valery Gerasimov, and other Russian leaders have employed disinformation to spread chaos for strategic effect," a recent study in *The American Interest* noted. "The Kremlin's goal is to create an environment in which the side that copes best with chaos (that is, which is less susceptible to societal disruption) wins. The premise is Huntingtonian: that Russia can endure in a clash of civilizations by splintering its opponents' alliances with each other, dividing them internally, and undermining their political systems."

Our foes prosper when we let partisan politics take up more airtime than the reporting on facts without prejudice.

We must, however, always continue to debate the serious issues that face this country. It is in this arena that social media can play a profoundly positive role. Instead of stoking the fires of division and hatred, the press could use analytics to find out which issues Americans are discussing on social media and present reasonable viewpoints from a variety of sources. For example, exit polls for the 2018 midterm elections clearly showed that health care was the most important factor for voters, yet where are the debates and studies being broadcast on TV about the topic? Let the American people drive what the media covers, not the media organization's bottom line.

Those in charge of major media organizations have a responsibility to publish rational, respectful voices. These voices can be from every walk of life with every political belief, so long as they stick to the issues at hand, and refrain from ad hominem attacks.

Journalism with Proof

The hallmark of journalism that the American people can trust is simply empirical proof. Anonymous sources play an extremely vital role in many important breaking news stories, given the sensitivity of material discussed, and not all stories can be written with the backbone of documentation. However, whenever possible, the press should provide the reader with the records, documents, correspondences, etc., that go into producing an investigative report. By lifting this veil of secrecy and becoming as transparent as possible with the reader, journalists can quickly silence cries of "fake news" and, more importantly, establish credibility and trustworthiness.

Whereas anonymous sources and "palace intrigue" stories can easily be written off as "fake news" because of the lack of empirical proof, data journalism with documentation is much more difficult to dispute. This will require a shift in approach by journalists, as most major publications have largely moved away from investigative reports and have opted to focus on news that attracts a wider pool of readers, but investing time and resources into deeply sourced investigative data journalism is the path forward. This may not be sexy in a world of 280-character tweets and forty-second news hits on TV, but it is the necessary road ahead to restoring the full potential of a free press in America and combatting those who seek to discredit it.

I have taken this approach in my reporting, perhaps to a fault, to give the reader a complete understanding of how the information for a story was acquired and why it matters. In my view, it is absolutely imperative that journalists show their work, so to speak, and actually print the documentation that forms the foundation of a news story. Of course, journalists must still protect their sources and not give away any human intelligence that could be compromising in any way. Apart from that consideration, though, there is no reason to withhold anything from the reader.

I faced this dilemma in late 2018 when I, along with my co-author Natasha Bertrand, had to weigh the need to show our work with the possible alienation of a source. I was able to get my hands on a document that had been sent to Representative Adam Schiff in November, wherein a person who represented themselves as being close to George Papadopoulos made a series of monumental claims about an alleged Russian business deal in 2016. Mr. Papadopoulos claimed, according to this source, that the deal would result in a large financial gain for himself and Mr. Trump and "set him up for life." However, the person who wrote the document ended it with, "I do not want this letter to be shared with the media or anyone beside your office and relevant committees."

The document that I was able to acquire was unredacted and therefore I was able to see the name of the author of the letter, as well as details that would give away his/her identity. After teaming up with Natasha, we had to make the decision of whether or not to publish the letter. On the one hand, I had the intense responsibility of not putting this source in any danger, as well as his/her request for the media to not share the letter. On the other hand, I felt that journalists have a duty to show their work in such a way that the reader feels confident that the reporting is factual.

In an effort to reconcile these two responsibilities that I felt, we ultimately had to compromise. First and foremost, the safety of an individual is the most important consideration in journalism. This can never be compromised, no matter how strong the desire to be transparent may be. Natasha and I came to the conclusion that the letter could be published so long as redactions protected any information that could be used to identify the source. I published the letter, with redactions, on my social media accounts and subsequently received scorn from both sides of the debate. Some thought that I should have heeded the person's wishes and not published the letter at all, while others wanted to see the letter without redactions. While I understood both arguments, I felt that the compromise kept my source safe and still lived up to the extremely high standards that I place on journalists.

Phrases in a news story such as "documents seen by the [insert news organization] depict . . ." only deepen the level of mistrust from the average citizen, as it feels like the news organization is secretly keeping information close to the chest. Furthermore, when phrases like this are used, there is a sense of arrogance, as if the reader isn't intelligent enough to understand the source documentation. It is my philosophy that, whenever possible, it is preferable to show the documents that I have reviewed, showing a certain level of trust with the reader that hopefully will be reciprocated in time. This can be a direct rebuke to those who want to falsely label a report as fake news. It is easy to claim that anonymous sources and "documents seen" but not printed are fake; it is nearly impossible to levy this charge when the whole world can see the underlying documentation.

Additionally, when discussing matters on-the-record with people who appear in a story, the press should consider publishing these discussions. This is yet another method to provide the public the highest level of transparency possible. The reader should be able to see as much of the process as possible in an effort to lend credence to the article and establish a level of openness. The American people are not stupid. In cases where sources and methods aren't at risk, there is absolutely no reason for the press to be deceptive with their audience.

It is incumbent upon dedicated journalists not only to ensure that their work is double, triple, and quadruple fact-checked, but also to show their findings in a transparent manner. In the same way that a high school math teacher might pressure students to show each step of how they arrived at an answer, journalists must be held accountable for telling the story while at the same time illustrating how the information for the story was acquired.

This process can take many different forms. The power of a screenshot of an email correspondence, for example, holds much more weight than simply printing the words. An audio recording of a telephone conversation (where legal) with a subject of an article is much more persuasive than a transcript of the discussion. A picture of a banking statement, a video of an incident, and a cut-out of a court document are all much more persuasive than a plain description of this source documentation.

The Role of Independent Journalism

Journalists independent from a news organization play a vital role in the ever-expanding world of open source intelligence. The amount of information that can be uncovered from hidden-yet-accessible open source research is incredible and sometimes overwhelming. Currently, news outlets are extremely hesitant to cite independent journalists on social media, as it represents a massive shift in the paradigm of reporting.

"Traditionally in this field, we give credit to full blown-stories, not tweets. That's the standards," an editor of a large news organization told me when I asked if he would be willing to acknowledge that I had tweeted out information before one of his senior writers wrote an "exclusive" piece containing the same data. The tweet was never cited.

This is not to garner sympathy for a newspaper failing to mention my work, but rather an insight into the reluctance of these companies to adapt to the times. Independent journalists can dig deep into congressional travel records, for example, with the same capability as a paid writer.

Too often, however, independent journalism gets hijacked by those who spread conspiracy theories that play to people's fears in the pursuit of fame, fortune, or some combination of both. All positions on the political spectrum can be and have been victim to these theories that seem plausible but don't rely on fact or evidence. In my view, this modern form of yellow journalism can be as destructive to the fabric of American society as those who persistently and publicly attack the free press.

The leap from political and investigative analysis to outlandish conspiracy theory is not as big as one might think. The power of social media has turned what used to be fringe conspiracy believers into a larger portion of the population. *If a post by someone with a blue check-mark is being shared or retweeted thousands of times, then it must have a hint of truth.* It is an easy trap to fall into, hearing what you want to hear instead of hearing what is actually true.

The Russia investigation, combined with the power of social media, has produced an immense wave of information from many sources. Part of the strategy from the Russian government in interfering with the 2016 election and beyond was to create chaos and confusion. In the indictment of the Russian "troll factory," Special Counsel Robert Mueller's office said that the Russians "had a strategic goal to sow discord in the U.S. political system, including the 2016 U.S. presidential election." The Russians organized Americans with many different political views. Part of the effort included funding both sides of the debate about the "Black Lives Matter" movement, resulting in protests and counter-protests that were both set up by the Russian operatives.

These foreign enemies seek to create an angry, divided American population. One of their main goals is to see the United States so preoccupied with internal strife that it cannot be seen as a global leader on important issues. If this chaotic America becomes so wrought with division, the Russians and others hope, then it will cease to be a great power in international affairs. Nations such as Russia, China, Iran, and others could then hypothetically fill the vacuum left by our country.

The media as a whole can play an extremely important role in ensuring that this vision of a divided America doesn't come to pass.

It is within this context that we all should strive to remain dedicated to fact and reason. Those who fabricate and disseminate false information for whatever purpose only bolster our foreign adversaries. A wild conspiracy theory about the Russia investigation, for instance, is a home run for the very Russian operatives who seek to divide us.

There are many public figures on social media and elsewhere who have become popular (and wealthy) for feigning inside information into the Mueller probe. Some even claim that members of Mr. Trump's campaign are going to face the death penalty for espionage crimes. "My sources say the death penalty, for espionage, being considered for @StevenKBannon," one such figure with hundreds of thousands of followers wrote in 2017. "I am pro-life and take no pleasure in reporting this."

Recognizing that these voices are doing precisely what our enemies dream of—sowing discord and chaos—is a point that cannot be overstated. If a claim based on anonymous sources seems like it might be too outlandish, it probably is. It's important to consistently identify and condemn people who spread conspiracy theories for personal gain. These grifters are willingly or unwillingly doing the bidding of foes who would love nothing more than to see America crumble from the internal political divisions among its citizens. Don't let them win.

Looking at the future of journalism, isolating and elevating independent researchers who show their work and do their due diligence instead of those who make up wild claims will be paramount. There is no doubt that the future of journalism is going to be much more of a team effort among regular citizens who focus on areas of investigations that news organizations can't or won't spend resources on. Separating fear-mongering from fact will allow this future to thrive.

The world needs sound investigative journalism to sort fact from fiction and shine light when and where those in power depend on enduring cloudiness. This journalism cannot simply be driven by entertainment, profits, or clicks, but by the principle that "whatever may be our wishes, our inclinations, or the dictates of our passion, they cannot alter the state of facts and evidence."

———

Through the lens of someone who grew up not knowing who in the public arena to trust, I made the decision to jump into the deep end of journalism with little prior experience. The overwhelming lack of evidence-based reporting, combined with a unique set of political circumstances that seemed crushing at times, drove the strong obligation that I felt to chip in with what I knew best: research and objectivity.

My past forays into writing were limited to baseball data analysis and terrorism studies, but something about the Russia investigation demanded that I participate in the fact-finding. Posting on Reddit and discussing current events with friends and family didn't feel like enough anymore, so when the first charges were brought by Special Counsel Robert Mueller and the effort by the Trump camp to downplay their significance was not met with resounding resistance based on the facts, I started a blog to chronicle the investigation wherever the evidence took me.

My reports on the Trump campaign's ties to Russia organically picked up steam, and after a year of investigative journalism, my follower count had incredibly soared passed 60,000. The idea of writing a book about my investigations was first broached to me by Skyhorse Publishing in September 2018, and we quickly sketched out an outline and agreed to work together.

I wrote this book in the hopes that someone who has never heard about the Russia investigation could pick it up and understand the premise, while also seeking to include fresh information for those who follow the probe closely. I've chosen to focus on the five main areas in which most of my work has been done and which constitute the broad foundations of the Trump-Russia conspiracy.

I still cannot believe that this opportunity has presented itself to me at such a young age. I am eternally grateful for all of those who have put up with my antics along the way.

Scott Stedman

Introduction

THE ELECTION OF DONALD TRUMP AS President of the United
States in 2016 came as a shock to nearly everyone who had an
interest in world politics. Pundits, pollsters, political scientists,
and writers had all forecast a win for his Democratic opponent Hillary
Clinton, leaving many asking *How did this happen?*

At least one branch of the many reasons that Mrs. Clinton ultimately lost the Electoral College became increasingly clear as the
2016 election reached its pinnacle.

One month before election day, the Department of Homeland
Security and Office of the Director of National Intelligence released a
joint statement saying in part that, "The U.S. Intelligence Community
(USIC) is confident that the Russian Government directed the recent
compromises of e-mails from US persons and institutions."

These emails, stolen from John Podesta, Mrs. Clinton's Campaign
Chairman, and other high-ranking officials of the Democratic National
Committee, were selectively leaked to publications such as WikiLeaks.
The content of the emails was covered breathlessly by major media
outlets, with seemingly none interested in the source of the information, despite pleas from Robby Mook, the Clinton Campaign Manager,
and Mrs. Clinton herself.

Though the impact that the release of the emails had on the outcome of the 2016 election can be debated, most political scientists

agree that it was at least one of the reasons why Mrs. Clinton lost when she was the odds-on favorite. What cannot be denied is that a foreign adversary stole information from one of the two major US political parties and released it to the public in a secretive way to influence the outcome of the presidential election. Not only are these acts highly illegal, but they compromise the integrity of the most sacred aspect of a functioning democracy: the right to vote. Americans deserve the privilege to decide who to elect without the one-sided influence of a foreign government. In 2016, this privilege was criminally stripped away from the average citizen.

No matter your political or social views, we must be united in recognizing that elections in the United States should be solely decided by its citizens, without the influence of any foreign entities. The successful effort by the Russian government to intrude in the American electoral process through a series of cybercrimes in 2016 is something that should anger all Americans, and indeed everyone around the world who believes in free and fair elections. One can debate the effectiveness of the actions taken by the Russian government, but the actions themselves deserve immense condemnation.

As was verified by nearly every intelligence agency in the country in January 2017, the Russian government interfered in the election by stealing emails from Mrs. Clinton's inner circle and the Democratic Party and releasing the information methodically in the months leading up to voting day. This effort was coupled with a massive propaganda push by Russian actors who targeted American voters with disinformation on social media. The Russian government undertook these cyberattacks in an attempt to help Mr. Trump's chances of becoming president, as he was a person who had for decades publicly and privately called for warmer relations with Russia and praised its autocratic leader, Vladimir Putin.

The wave of disinformation and confusion regarding the events of 2016 is an ongoing battle in all forms of media. Despite this, however, there are truths about the Russian cyberattack on our democratic processes that cannot be denied. It is crucial now more than ever that we as a public stick to the facts and evidence that can rise above any attempts to muddy the waters.

The Russian cyberattack on the 2016 election began in earnest in the summer of 2015, when the Russian intelligence-connected hacker group nicknamed "Cozy Bear" successfully infiltrated the Democratic National Committee's (DNC) computer systems. This gave the Russian hackers access to top Democrats' emails, chats, and other confidential information. In the spring of 2016, Cozy Bear had company within the DNC systems in the form of the Russian military intelligence hacker group Fancy Bear. Whereas Cozy Bear seemed to be more interested in long-term spying and intelligence collection, Fancy Bear had a different motive: to help elect Donald Trump by splintering the Democratic Party and damaging Hillary Clinton.

Fancy Bear also managed to penetrate the email account of John Podesta, chairman of Mrs. Clinton's presidential campaign. They disseminated this stolen information to outfits of "plausible deniability" such as WikiLeaks and an online persona called "Guccifer 2.0," through which the Russian government could deny knowledge of the hacking. In reality, WikiLeaks and Guccifer 2.0 acted as an arm of the hostile Kremlin attack on the US presidential election.

The majority of the private DNC emails were released through Guccifer 2.0, who falsely claimed to be a lone Romanian hacker instead of its true identity: Russian military intelligence. Mr. Podesta's emails were gradually and methodically released by WikiLeaks, oftentimes within minutes of negative stories about Mr. Trump being published.

The Trump–Russia investigation was officially initiated in mid-2016, when the FBI got word that at least one Trump associate had had foreknowledge that Russia had "dirt" on Hillary Clinton in the form of damaging emails. After FBI Director James Comey was fired by President Trump in May 2017, a Special Counsel was soon named. Robert Mueller, a Vietnam war hero, longtime prosecutor, and Mr. Comey's predecessor as FBI Director, was called upon by the Deputy Attorney General to investigate "any links and/or coordination between the Russian government and individuals associated with the campaign of President Donald Trump."

In the months following Mr. Mueller's appointment as Special Counsel, there has been an avalanche of information dropped on the public regarding the numerous connections that the Trump campaign had with Russian officials, operatives, and intelligence agents. The goal posts for those in Mr. Trump's inner circle have moved tremendously since word first broke that authorities were investigating his ties to Russia.

"There was no communication between the campaign and any foreign entity during the campaign," Trump's spokeswoman Hope Hicks definitively proclaimed in late 2016. Vice President-elect Mike Pence went on Fox News in January of 2017 and was asked, "Was there any contact in any way between Trump or his associates and the Kremlin or cutouts they had?" Mr. Pence replied, "Of course not. Why would there be any contacts between the campaign?

Since these statements, at least ninety-four contacts between members of the Trump campaign and transition and Russian-linked operatives have surfaced, according to a study done by the Moscow Project. At least thirteen members of the Trump team, as well as multiple Trump business associates, had contact with Russians during the campaign, and numerous others were aware of these contacts.

Some of the communications with Russians were with private citizens, but others took place directly with the Russian government. Undeniably, an extensive coverup ensued to hide these communications with the very entity that had waged a cyberattack against Mr. Trump's opponents.

The media as a whole struggled to keep up with the important details of the relationship between the Trump campaign and Russian individuals. The overwhelming amount of evidence that was being dropped on the public hourly meant that, among other things, the larger picture of the Trump-Russia story became a behemoth that was difficult to keep up with for even the most avid political-news consumer.

Real News attempts to break through this chaos and concisely present the five main areas in which Mr. Trump and his associates are linked to Russia:

1. The negotiations to build Trump Tower Moscow, which were conducted during the most crucial months of Mr. Trump's campaign.

2. Two secret meetings in Trump Tower in Manhattan, in which election help was promised to the Trump campaign by foreign entities.
3. The story of Trump adviser George Papadopoulos, who was the first to learn about Russian dirt on Hillary Clinton, and his new wife, who attempted to make matters still more chaotic.
4. The successful infiltration of the National Rifle Association by a Russian banker and his young female operative.
5. Suspicious activity involving those in the Trump campaign, including secret overnight flights, business transactions, and a public confession of collusion by a well-known Kremlin propagandist.

With limited resources and connections in the political world, I took a different tack than most major news organizations. I relied heavily on documents, official records, and open-source intelligence to strongly diminish the possibility of being disregarded as fake news. One can easily denounce anonymous sources as false, but it becomes nearly impossible to dilute the power of investigative journalism when the proof from tangible documentation is printed in black-and-white.

My lodestar throughout my year-plus of investigations was this simple, prescient-yet-powerful declaration by the second President of the United States, John Adams:

"Facts are stubborn things; and whatever may be our wishes, our inclinations, or the dictates of our passion, they cannot alter the state of facts and evidence."

Trump Tower Moscow and Dirty Russian Money

Who's Who:
- **Michael Cohen:** Mr. Trump's longtime lawyer and "fixer." Vice President of the Trump Organization.
- **Felix Sater:** Russian mob-connected real estate developer and former assistant to Mr. Trump. Cooperated and provided valuable information to the FBI in counter-terrorism cases.
- **Andrey Rozov:** Moscow based real estate developer who has been associated with Mr. Sater for nearly a decade.

Overview

In the midst of his presidential run, Donald Trump signed a letter of intent to build the tallest building in Europe. The ambitious Moscow plan, orchestrated and negotiated by Mr. Trump's longtime lawyer and fixer, Michael Cohen, would have put Mr. Trump's name atop one of the largest buildings in the world, towering over every other structure in Russia. The negotiations extended well into 2016, a fact that Mr. Cohen attempted to cover-up with repeated lies stating that the project was terminated in January of that year.

His actions in attempting to secure the real estate transaction have garnered the intense interest of Mr. Mueller as he investigates the various contacts between the Trump campaign and Russian entities. In late November 2018, Mr. Cohen pleaded guilty to lying to Congress about the Trump Tower Moscow project. He was sentenced to three years in prison for his lies to Congress, as well as a slew of financial crimes.

The prospect of partnering with a Russian developer during the presidential campaign was first brought to the attention of the Trump organization by the enigmatic character of Felix Sater. Mr. Sater, a convicted felon for his role in a bar fight and participation in a Russian mafia-backed stock-fraud scheme in the 2000s, is one of the most intriguing players in the Trump-Russia story.

Mr. Sater's connections to the Russian mafia extend far past the Wall Street fraud. His father was, according to FBI agents, a crime boss for the Russian don, Semion Mogilevich, who has been dubbed "the most dangerous mobster in the world."

After his arrests in the early 2000s, however, Mr. Sater became a key figure in combating foreign enemies around the world as an asset for the CIA and FBI. "[Sater] provided the United States highly sensitive information concerning various terrorists and rogue states," Loretta Lynch, then-US Attorney, wrote in a 2011 sealed court document. Following the September 11th, 2001 attacks on New York and Washington DC, Sater traveled to the Middle East and provided the United States crucial intelligence about al-Qaeda and its affiliates.

Mr. Sater continued to provide intelligence to federal authorities for years, including information about Russian organized crime, money laundering, and even Osama Bin Laden. His cooperation has led to major successes for the United States government in their efforts to protect the country and bring down some of the world's most notorious criminals.

"I have no problem with truth it's only when I get referred to as a margarita glass wielding Trump russian gangster partner that truly upsets me and hurts my family for no apparent reason other than to write salacious crap about Donald Trump using me as a whipping boy," Sater told me exclusively via email. "Especially given my service and sacrifice for our country."

Mr. Sater, who also cooperated with federal investigators investigating the stock-fraud case in order to avoid prison time, was a senior adviser to Mr. Trump for years in the late 2000s, after Mr. Sater's Bayrock Group partnered with the Trump Organization to build

Trump SoHo, a condominium complex in Manhattan. Trump SoHo attracted a plethora of Russian buyers and was mired in allegations of money laundering and fraud. No one involved was ever convicted of a crime relating to the project.

"With our project in SoHo . . . we see a lot of money pouring in from Russia," stated Donald Trump Jr. in 2008, just as construction for the new condo complex was completed. The comments by Mr. Trump Jr. came as a high-profile Russian oligarch named Dmitry Rybolovlev purchased a Trump mansion in Florida for $95,000,000, a profit of over $54,000,000 for Mr. Trump in less than three years. Mr. Rybolovlev never stepped foot in the home, and later began selling part of the land.

During the campaign, Mr. Trump attempted to distance himself from Mr. Sater, saying that he wouldn't recognize Mr. Sater if he were in the room. Behind the scenes, however, Mr. Sater was acting as a key liaison between the Trump team and Russian banks, government officials, and spies.

Chronicled in a series of investigative reports by *BuzzFeed* and later corroborated by others, the Trump Tower Moscow saga stretched well into the 2016 campaign season, with Mr. Sater holding out hope for a deal until late July.

Just weeks after Mr. Trump announced his candidacy, Mr. Sater reached out to his childhood friend Mr. Cohen, proposing that the Trump Organization partner with a Russian real-estate developer called IC Expert to build Trump World Tower Moscow. Mr. Sater knew IC Expert's principal, Andrey Rozov, from their days working for a major Russian real-estate conglomerate.

Mr. Rozov, not regarded as an oligarch with significant political power, was an unlikely choice to partner with the Trump Organization. In years prior, the Trump team had discussed building in Moscow with some of the most influential Russians close to President Putin, including Aras Agalarov. Now, in the middle of his campaign for president, Mr. Trump signed a letter-of-intent to build Trump World Tower Moscow with a less-experienced, second-tier developer.

Rozov and his company, IC Expert, only had a few major developments in Russia under their belt. The main project built by IC Expert was a complex known as Novokosino.

The Novokosino development, which primarily consisted of apartment buildings, was anything but a success. IC Expert failed to deliver many of the units on time, which led to dozens of lawsuits from investors and prospective homeowners, many of whom lost hundreds of thousands of dollars. To this day, not all of the construction is completed, some seven years after the building began.

Mr. Rozov himself has a checkered past. In 2011, he was charged with negligent homicide after recklessly causing a boat crash that resulted in the death of a nineteen-year-old man and seriously injured his girlfriend. Mr. Rozov was later granted amnesty by the Russian government (as detailed later in this chapter) and all charges were dropped.

Still, the Trump Organization decided that Mr. Rozov and IC Expert were suitable partners. Mr. Sater vouched for IC Expert and thought that Mr. Rozov would be able to pull off the daunting task of building Trump Tower Moscow.

"I am friends with Andrey for over a decade, he is a great developer," Sater told me. "It would have been extremely easy to do the development with him. Just 2 friends trying to pull together a huge deal. In hindsight a terrible mistake which threw us into this gutter of news, slime and conspiracy theories."

Mr. Cohen and Mr. Sater discussed not only the real-estate venture in Moscow, but also a possible meeting between Mr. Putin and then-candidate Trump. At the invitation of Dmitry Peskov, one of Mr. Putin's closest deputies, Mr. Cohen planned to travel to the St. Petersburg International Economic Forum in June.

Mr. Peskov "wants to meet there with you and possibly introduce you to either Putin or Medvedev," Mr. Sater wrote in an email to Mr. Cohen.

"Works for me," Mr. Cohen said.

But when it came time to get their visas from the Russian consulate in New York, Mr. Cohen unexpectedly and abruptly postponed the trip. He wanted to go to Russia after the Republican National Convention (RNC) in July, he said.

Intriguingly, Mr. Cohen did end up traveling abroad before the RNC: the week preceding the convention, he flew to Italy for what he says was a family vacation. It remains unclear why Mr. Cohen thought the Russia trip before the RNC was untenable, but his nine-day Italian vacation was acceptable. Both he and Mr. Sater publicly maintain that the Italy trip was simply time spent relaxing with his family.

Negotiations between the Trump Organization and various Russian banks to finance the project were conducted via Sater, the shadowy figure with connections to both American intelligence and high-profile Russian businessmen and politicians. Mr. Sater relied on a contact who spent years in the GRU, the foreign military intelligence agency of the Armed Forces of the Russian Federation. The "former" spy (Mr. Sater has acknowledged that he doesn't believe that spies in Russia ever cease their operations) has yet to be named in any press reports.

The banks that offered to finance Trump Tower Moscow, according to Mr. Sater, were VTB Bank, at first, and then later GenBank. Mr. Cohen was allegedly offended that Mr. Sater would turn to GenBank, an institution that Mr. Cohen saw as "third-tier."

"After almost two months of waiting you send me some bullshit letter from a third-tier bank and you think I'm going to walk into the boss's office and tell him I'm going there for this?" Mr. Cohen wrote to Mr. Sater. "Tell them no thank you and I will take it from here."

While this negotiating was taking place, however, IC Expert was securing huge sums of money from Russia's largest bank—Sberbank. My research would show that the development company led by Mr. Rozov received a loan of 10.6 billion rubles, some $162 million, just days after the Letter-of-Intent was signed by Mr. Trump. After this loan was issued, the Novokosino project didn't see a great increase in construction activity and IC Expert didn't embark on any new developments. Where this money ended up remains a question mark.

Major media reporting didn't investigate IC Expert or Rozov thoroughly. My months-long investigation into IC Expert and Andrey Rozov revealed that not only was the Russian government involved in the effort to a certain extent, but that the money-managers of IC Expert were previously involved in schemes of money laundering, fraud, and other financial crimes.

Though Mr. Rozov claimed to be the sole owner of IC Expert, the ownership structure told a different story. Clearly set up to obfuscate the actual owners, the corporate structure of IC Expert ran through three offshore locations. Without knowing who was behind these off-shore accounts, the Trump Organization had no idea with whom it was truly doing business.

The Process

My first three reports on Trump Tower Moscow came in quick succession and relied on open-source information and charts and maps to connect the dots to make sense of it all. I wanted to learn more about the background of Andrey Rozov, as well as the money trail behind IC Expert.

The files from Russia were voluminous, detailed, and daunting to sort through. Over twenty-five different documents showed the company's financials, articles of incorporation, officials in charge, and shareholders. One file, though, caught my eye, because it was in a category of its own: charges and mortgages.

The document showed that Sberbank had issued a line of credit to IC Expert in November 2015 worth up to nearly 10.6 billion rubles, approximately 162 million dollars at the time.

Ποσό που διασφαλίστηκε με την Επιβάρυνση	Μέχρι και το ποσό των 10,595,900,000.00 Ρουβλιών (δέκα δισεκατομμύρια πεντακόσια ενενήντα πέντε εκατομμύρια εννιακόσιες χιλιάδες ρούβλια) που οφείλονται από την Expert LLC στην Sberbank δυνάμει της Συμφωνίας Πίστωσης. Up to the amount of 10,595,900,000.00 RUB (ten billion five hundred ninety five million nine hundred thousand rubles) owed by Expert LLC to Sberbank pursuant to the Credit Line Agreement.

The timing of this line-of-credit was incredibly suspect. For a development company with a small portfolio to suddenly have access to such an enormous amount of money from a state-owned bank, just twenty-one days after signing a preliminary deal with Donald Trump, raised all sorts of red flags.

At the time, Mr. Trump was surging in the polls. The opening paragraph to a story printed by CNN five days before the Sberbank loan was issued read, "Donald Trump has a double-digit lead over Ben Carson in the Republican presidential race and voters say they prefer change over political experience, two new national polls show."

Sberbank, whose main owner is the Central Bank of Russia, making it a Russian-government entity, decided to fully fund an inexperienced development company who just days prior partnered with the leading Republican contender to be the President of the United States. The line-of-credit appeared to be a form of the Russian government encouraging IC Expert and their efforts to build Trump Tower Moscow.

This financing was the basis of my first report on the subject.

December 1, 2017
Exclusive: Developer of Trump Tower Moscow Received Loan from Sanctioned Sberbank Three Weeks After Signing Letter of Intent
IC Expert Investment Company Owners Include Three Mystery LLCs Located in Cyprus and the Marshall Islands; Chairman Was Charged with Negligent Homicide in 2011.

The developer of Trump Tower Moscow received a non-revolving line of credit from the U.S.-sanctioned Sberbank three weeks after signing a Letter of Intent (LOI) with Trump Acquisitions LLC. A letter of intent describes the details of a real estate transaction before it is finalized. The agreement was signed by Donald Trump on October 28th, 2015, four months into his presidential run.

A non-revolving credit line is typically in the form of an installment loan, which is given in a lump sum and then paid back over regular installments with interest assessed. This means that money was being borrowed by IC Expert from the state-owned Sberbank. Previously, Trump Organization lawyer Michael Cohen claimed that the deal fell through in January 2016, after he lost confidence that the firm could secure financing.

An analysis of banking, financial, and tax records shows that IC Expert received a non-revolving line of credit from Sberbank on November 18th, 2015. The company pledged 100% of its equity to secure the 10.6-billion-ruble credit line, indicating a level of significance.

The records have also uncovered the shadowy owners behind IC Expert—a complex web of both Russian and offshore shell companies whose frequent changes of ownership, directors, company names and addresses effectively obfuscates their financial dealings. The company's current ownership is registered to three LLCs, with 85% of the ownership shared between two offshore companies located in Cyprus and the Marshall Islands.

The shareholders in the company as of 2015 included Colinsen Trading Limited, a Cyprus-based LLC with 60% share in IC Expert, Trianguli Limited, a Marshall Islands LLC with 25% share, and "EKOPRESTIZH", a Russian LLC with 15% share.

In a written statement released in September by Trump's lawyer Michael

Cohen, he claimed that, "In late January 2016, I abandoned the Moscow proposal because I lost confidence that the prospective licensee would be able to obtain the real estate, financing and government approvals necessary to bring the proposal to fruition."

With these new revelations, Mr. Cohen's statement appears misleading. Sberbank is Russia's largest state-owned bank. A pledge of 100% of the company equity for the line of credit suggests that not only was IC Expert well on its way to obtaining the financing needed for site selection, regulatory work, etc., but it also had a degree of confidence from Putin's government.

In 2014, after the annexation of Crimea, the US and EU imposed sanctions on many Russian institutions, including Sberbank. These sanctions barred companies from dealing in any debt Sberbank issued of longer than thirty days' maturity.

Andrey Rozov, the IC Expert Chairman and Trump LOI signatory, founded the company in 2005. The company's first project was awarded in 2011 for a residential development project called Novokosino-2 in the city of Reutov, a suburb of Moscow. Sberbank appears to have provided the initial financing for the project, as well.

That same year, Rozov was involved in a fatal boating accident in the harbor of Crocus City. Rozov was charged with negligent homicide, yet the case stalled and it is unclear what became of the charges.

By the end of 2014, IC Expert had become mired in scandal over its failure to construct thousands of apartment units paid for by home buyers. The Novokosino project has required ongoing intervention by local and regional government officials to address the growing protests of co-investors. Even under this supposed government supervision, many of the buildings—first promised in July 2015 and then December 2015—still remain under construction.

Yet in 2015, Rozov's scandal-plagued IC Expert was looking to expand into the luxury skyscrapers sector in Moscow. The licensing deal with Trump was predicated on the firm's ability to secure financing, land, and government permission. It included an initial $4 million dollar 'upfront' payment to 'Trump Acquisition LLC and/or one or more of its affiliates.' It is unclear whether such a payment was ever made.

The project was deemed so "important" to Cohen that in January 2016, he reached out to Putin's spokesperson Peskov for help. In that email,

Cohen wrote, "without getting into lengthy specifics, the communication between our two sides has stalled."

Trump's lawyer, Marc Kasowitz, is the lead defense counsel for Sberbank in a Manhattan case. During Trump's trip to Moscow in 2013, he met with the Sberbank CEO Herman Gref. "There was a good feeling from the meeting," Gref said in an interview. "He's a sensible person, very lively in his responses, with a positive energy and a good attitude toward Russia."

The deal signed by Trump and his lawyer Michael Cohen offers no signs that they properly vetted IC Expert. Neither mystery offshore owners nor a homicide appears to have deterred them from signing the Letter of Intent. Doing business deals with shady characters in foreign countries opens political candidates up to potentially being compromised. This material can be held against the political figure in order to ensure loyalty.

Kasowitz and Cohen did not return requests for comment.

———————

After learning that the Russian state, via Sberbank, was funding IC Expert, I decided to dive into any connections that Mr. Rozov might have with the Russian government. Searching Mr. Rozov's name in Russian, Андрей Розов, led me to a blog titled "Murder, shareholders, Trump Tower." With a title like that, how can one not read the article?

The article, written by a community activist in Russia, made a series of claims that ended up being half-verifiable, half-uncorroborated. The main assertion was that Mr. Rozov was charged with negligent homicide in 2011 after a boating accident outside of Moscow. Attempting to verify this story, I began searching through Russian court records in an effort to find the underlying documents about the case.

Records from a Moscow City Court confirmed the charges against Mr. Rozov and the fact that amnesty issued by the Russian government was applied to the case, absolving Mr. Rozov of any wrongdoing. Coupled with the loan from the Russian state-owned Sberbank, it became clear that the Russian government knew about Rozov and his deal with Mr. Trump.

This intervention by the Russian government, weeks before Mr. Trump would announce his candidacy, was the basis for my December 4, 2017 report.

December 4, 2017
Russian Government Granted Amnesty to the Chairman of the Trump Tower Moscow Development Company

On April 24, 2015, Andrey Rozov, accused of negligent homicide, was granted amnesty by way of Government Proclamation.

In the leadup to Donald Trump's announcement of his presidential bid in Spring 2015, the Russian Government granted amnesty to Andrey Rozov, the Chairman of IC Expert, who four months later would sign a Letter of Intent (LOI) to build Trump Tower in Moscow City. Rozov was accused of negligent homicide in the death of a nineteen-year-old man.

Official court records, translated by Indiana University alumnus Lorenz Cohen, a Russian speaker, show that hundreds of defendants were granted amnesty by the State Duma in the early morning hours of April 24, 2015. In the same hour that the order of amnesty was released, Trump retweeted at least seven supporters encouraging him to run for President.

Four days later, on April 28, a Moscow City Court officially applied the amnesty to Rozov's case. Prosecutors alleged that Rozov was recklessly driving his speed boat when he crashed into a smaller boat, killing the man and seriously injuring a twenty-three-year-old female.

The court records also show that an appeal by one of the victims was denied on June 17, 2015, the same day that Donald Trump announced his candidacy for President. Three weeks later, as Trump was taking the lead in the polls for GOP primary, a regional judge appointed by President Putin in 2002 upheld the lower court decision to clear Rozov of all charges.

The intervention of the Russian government in a case where the defendant was facing years in prison raises new questions about the extent of Putin's involvement in the proposed Trump Tower Moscow deal. Previously, Trump's lawyer, Michael Cohen, suggested that he emailed Kremlin Spokesman Dmitry Peskov in order to seek the Russian government's help to move the project along.

Last week it was discovered that in November of 2015, Russia's largest state-owned bank, Sberbank, approved a loan to IC Expert just three weeks after signing an LOI with Trump Organization for a luxury hi-rise tower in Moscow City. This fact, coupled with the involvement of the Russian government in clearing Rozov of any charges, suggests that the email to Peskov wasn't genuine. At least two arms of the Russian government, the judiciary and the state-owned Sberbank, made decisions that allowed Trump and Cohen to pursue the deal.

Earlier this year, Michael Cohen had stated that he "abandoned the Moscow proposal because [he] lost confidence that the prospective licensee would be able to obtain the real estate, financing and government approvals necessary to bring the proposal to fruition."

The previously undisclosed loan, coupled with a grant of amnesty just six months prior to the deal, suggests that Cohen's statements are not accurate.

IC Expert currently faces dozens of accusations from investors and homeowners who say their homes and buildings are unfinished more than two years after their promised completion.

––––––––––

The Letter of Intent was the outcome of a Russian-born Trump adviser's quest to, "help world peace and make a lot of money." Felix Sater, a former business partner and senior adviser to Donald Trump, acted as an intermediary between the Russians and the Trump team to bring Trump's brand to Moscow. Sater and Rozov previously served together on the executive board of a real estate company called Mirax-Group until the company was liquidated and rebranded in 2011.

In 2011, Mirax-Group also received a loan from Sberbank to build the "tallest building in Europe," to the tune of $370 million. The founder of Mirax-Group, Sergei Polonsky, was found guilty of two cases of major fraud and embezzlement in 2017. State prosecutors alleged that he stole "more than 5.7 billion rubles (now $94 million) of prepayments for flats in an unfinished Moscow complex it was building."

Felix Sater also has a long and storied history with law enforcement. In 1991, he stabbed a man in the face with a margarita glass and ended up serving fifteen months in prison. In 1998 he pleaded guilty and became an FBI informant to a $40 million stock-fraud scheme orchestrated by the Russian Mafia.

He and his real-estate firm, Bayrock Group, partnered with Donald Trump in 2006 to build Trump SoHo. When the building was finished in 2010, Sater was a senior advisor to Donald Trump. The Bayrock office was located just two floors below the Trump Organization headquarters in Trump Tower. Alan Garten, a senior Trump Organization attorney, told ABC News in August that "there's really no direct relationship" between Sater and the Trump organization. Yet, in 2010, Felix Sater had his own personal business card with a Trump Organization email and the title "Senior Advisor to Donald Trump."

In a 2013 deposition, Trump claimed, "If [Sater] were sitting in the room right now I really wouldn't know what he looked like." When Trump was asked about his connections to Sater by the BBC in 2015, Trump stood up and left the room mid-interview.

The connections to Sater, Rozov, and the mystery offshore companies in Cyprus and the Marshall Islands that own IC Expert leave Trump unprotected from those who wish to obtain blackmail information on the businessman-turned-President. When connected to an adversarial government, this blackmail could be used to influence policy on a global scale.

The condensed timeline of the Rozov case in parallel to Trump's activities is below.

April 24, 2015

- A proclamation of amnesty is declared by the Russian State Duma. This amnesty will be applied to the Rozov case.
- Trump engages on Twitter, retweeting supporters who encourage him to run for President
- Trump gives keynote address to the Chesterfield GOP in Virginia, where he states, "If I run and if I win, this country will not be ripped off anymore."

April 29, 2015
- Moscow (Krasnogorsk) City Court terminates the case of Andrey Rozov by applying the amnesty proclamation to his case.
- Trump, at event in Iowa, says, "We have to fix the country. It's ill. It's not feeling well. It's been mistreated. It's been scoffed at. It's been run by incompetent people. It's been run by dishonest and crooked people. . . . It's been treated badly, and it needs help, and it needs it quickly."
- Trump again retweets multiple users, indicating he is running for President

June 16, 2015
- Donald Trump announces run for President
- Moscow Regional Court upholds the lower court's decision to clear Rozov.

––––––––––

Tracking the ownership structure of IC Expert unveiled a plethora of information. Like many Russian businesses, the trail ended up in offshore accounts in Cyprus, the Marshall Islands, and the British Virgin Islands. The latter two locations are nearly impossible for investigators without subpoena power to retrieve any information, as the secrecy laws in those countries are among the most strict in the world. Cyprus, however, is a bit more open.

The first batch of information I received was the basics—the name and address history of the shell company that owned the majority of IC Expert. Again, by simply using the power of various iterations of the addresses in a Google search, I was able to uncover previous accounts of fraud and money laundering at the exact same location.

––––––––––

December 8, 2017
Trump Tower Moscow Developer Used Same P.O. Box as Russian Oligarch Who Laundered Hundreds of Millions

A Cyprus company that stands to receive 60% of the profits from IC Expert, the developer that signed the 2015 Letter of Intent to build Trump Tower Moscow, was once registered at the same address as a Russian oligarch who laundered hundreds of millions of dollars.

Colinsen Trading Limited LLC's legal address was once located at 12 Kennedy Business Center, 2nd Floor, P.O. Box 1703, in Nicosia, Cyprus, according to official financial documents. The Kennedy Business Center is a modest six-story building in the Cypriot capital. Various companies use the Kennedy Business Center's offices and the use of the building is not nefarious in and of itself.

The exact same address, down to the floor and P.O. box number, was used by a shell company owned by Russian oligarch Sergei Pugachev, who laundered more than $200 million through the Cyprus company. According to the Russian government, Pugachev used the bank he co-founded to loan his own companies large amounts of money, knowing that the loans would never be repaid. In all, more than $2 billion was laundered.

The company in question, Diagoras Nominees Limited, acted as an intermediary for Pugachev to disperse the money to dozens of companies. It is registered at 12 Kennedy Business Center, 2nd Floor, P.O. Box 1703, in Nicosia, Cyprus. Pugachev fled to London and then to Nice, France to avoid prosecution by the Russian government. In July, Switzerland opened a money laundering investigation into Pugachev, and in October the UK High Court ruled that the former "Kremlin banker" sheltered wealth in offshore accounts with intention to mislead. Russia still seeks his extradition.

The revelation comes as more suspicious details about IC Expert, the developer with whom Trump and Michael Cohen signed a Letter of Intent to build Trump Tower Moscow in October 2015, are uncovered. Andrey Rozov founded the company in 2005, while he served on the board of Mirax, a real estate company whose owner also fled Russia amid accusations of fraud and money laundering. Early records show that Rozov's company was originally 99.9% owned by Colinsen Trading Limited.

The Letter of Intent was signed by Donald Trump four months into his Presidential bid. At this point, he was leading in the Republican primary polls by a healthy margin. To enter into a major real estate licensing deal with a company so mired in scandal and mystery left him tremendously vulnerable to being compromised. Publicly available records and a modest amount of investigating have revealed many red flags of which Trump and his team should have been aware.

First, it has been revealed that Andrey Rozov killed a man in 2011 by recklessly crashing his boat, and was later granted amnesty by the Russian government as Donald Trump was teasing his Presidential ambitions. Second, the mysterious offshore companies mean that anyone could have benefited from this deal. Third, mass allegations of fraud against the developer established that they had a less-than-admirable track record in Russia.

Now, the direct link to a major money laundering scheme raises serious questions as to why Trump didn't cease all negotiations with this company.

IC Expert's ownership has changed numerous times since 2005. Colinsen currently owns a 60% stake in the company, along with two other offshore LLCs whose owners have not yet been identified. The entire proceeds of IC Expert end up in offshore accounts.

The company's only major development complex, Novokosino-2, is still under construction. The Novokosino project has been mired in scandal for years. While the first set of buildings was delivered on time in 2013, construction had essentially stalled by 2014. Thousands of co-investors were left with no homes and no answers, prompting an intervention by regional government officials. Many of the buildings—first promised in July 2015 and then December 2015—still remain unfinished. Dozens of charges of fraud have been filed in regional courts, as IC Expert has claimed that they do not have the money to finish the construction.

It was recently discovered that three weeks after the Letter of Intent was signed, the three offshore owners pledged 100% of their equity in exchange for a loan from the state-owned Sberbank. This loan, as well as claimed assets worth more than $400 million, have investors and prospective home buyers furious and confused as to how the company has not been able to pay for the construction.

The risk of being in business with such sketchy actors is monumental for any political candidate. Trump and Michael Cohen, in the pursuit of financial gain, made themselves vulnerable to potential blackmail. It is unclear why they felt this risk was worth taking.

––––––––––

Oftentimes in Russian commerce, large companies like IC Expert are officially "owned" by a lawyer in another country in order to protect the identities of the true owners. These lawyers are called "nominal owners," as they don't actually own the company, but rather hold shares for their wealthy Russian clients. In turn, these lawyers get a small cut of the profits, which can still add up to millions of dollars.

The purchased business documents from the Cypriot government for the main shareholder of IC Expert—a shell company by the name of Colinsen Trading Limited—showed that a Cypriot lawyer by the name of Christodoulos Vassiliades was the nominal owner. Mr. Vassiliades, my research would show, represents some of the most powerful Russian clients in the political and business worlds.

Scouring business registries led me to find that his previous clients included the wife of notorious Russian mobster Semion Mogilevich and numerous Russian billionaires, such as Vladimir Lisin, Suleiman Kerimov, Alisher Usmanov, and others.

Mr. Vassiliades and his proxies in Cyprus were also connected to multiple instances of financial crimes, including money laundering. My profile on Mr. Vassiliades, including his connections to the Russian government and members of the Trump team, comprised my fourth report on Trump Tower Moscow.

I wrote this article on the campus of UC Irvine, during a lecture on voting and political manipulation. It seemed fitting.

––––––––––

December 19, 2017
Trump's Moscow Developer Owned by Bank of Cyprus Lawyer With Documented Money Laundering Ties

A prominent Cypriot lawyer known for serving Russian interests owns at least 60% of IC Expert, the Russian company Trump did business with during his presidential campaign.

Newly-obtained financial documents reveal that the Russian development company that signed a Letter-of-Intent (LOI) with Donald Trump during his presidential run is at least 60% owned by a Bank of Cyprus lawyer involved in alleged money-laundering operations for the Russian mob boss Semion Mogilevich and Russian oligarch Suleiman Kerimov.

In the 2015 LOI signed between IC Expert and Trump Acquisition LLC, IC Expert Chairman Andrey Rozov falsely certified that he owned 100% of the company. As was recently reported, IC Expert is actually owned by three "mystery" offshore companies—two in Cyprus and one in the Marshall Islands.

Principal:	Licensee hereby represents and warrants that the principal of Licensee is Andrey Rozov ("**Principal**"), who owns 100% of
	4
	A·R
Licensee.	COHEN_MICHAEL-00196443

Andrey Rozov claimed to own 100% of IC Expert

These new financial documents and open-source intelligence prove that at least one of IC Expert's Cyprus-based owners, Colinsen Trading Limited, is owned by Christodoulos Vassiliades—a high-profile Cypriot lawyer with links to the governments of Cyprus and Russia, and to the Bank of Cyprus.

Vassiliades's proximity to the Cyprus and Russian governments is well-documented. He and the daughter of the Cyprus President, Nicos Anastasiades, worked as Directors for the President's law firm. Vassiliades

Name	IONICS NOMINEES LIMITED			
Registration number	HE 134010			
Type	Company			
Subcategory	Private			
Name Status	Last Name			
Registration date	04/11/2002			
State of the Agency	Registered			
Status Date				
Goals	Business consultants and others.			

Date Last Post HE32   31/12/2015

Date of Last Change .01/01/2008

◉ Today   ○ Record

Form .Automatic Conversion of Share Capital from CYP to EURO

Today

Class of Shares	Number of Shares		Coin	Share Value
Nominal capital				
Nominal Fund EUR 8,550.00 divided as follows				
COMPLETE	5.000		EUR	1.71
Issued Capital				
Issued Fund EUR 1,710.00 divided as follows				
COMPLETE	1,000		EUR	1.71

Shareholders

- CHRISTODOULOS G. VASILEIADIS

Address

Diroanis, 10
Engomi
, Nicosia Cyprus

Details			
Class of Shares	Number of Shares	Coin	Share Value
COMPLETE	1,000	EUR	1.71

Chain of ownership leading to Christodoulos Vassiliades

and his law firm have also hosted numerous events for Anastasiades and high-ranking officials in the government.

During the Bank of Cyprus bailout in 2013 that cost Russian oligarchs billions in investments, Vassiliades was personally nominated by the head of the Bank of Moscow (now VTB) to become a shareholder in the Bank of Cyprus. The Russian bank was given this power as part of an effort to "bail-in" Russian investors by awarding them shares in the bank. Vassiliades's 8.37% share was valued at approximately $350 million. Records show that this share was reduced to 5.77% in 2014, and it is unclear what Vassiliades's current share in the bank may be.

Earlier that same year, an investigation by Russian financial daily *Vedomotsi* revealed that Vasilliades's law firm was appointed by the Bank of Cyprus to determine the validity and legality of foreign client operations, such as bank transfers. The report described Vasilliades's role as a guarantor of capital safety who helped foreigners pass compliance procedures and formalize the ownership structure of assets. The firm was recognized in 2015 for having "helped [consolidate] excellent relations between the Republic of Cyprus and the Russian Federation."

Vassiliades obtained 60% ownership of IC Expert through his Cyprus-based company Ionics Nominees Limited. Ownership of the company was transferred to Ionics Nominees in May 2015, days after Rozov was given amnesty by the Kremlin for a negligent homicide charge.

The designated Secretary of Ionics is Pampina Votsi, a Vassiliades Director connected to multiple cases of tax evasion, embezzlement, and money laundering for at least two high-profile Russians—Semion Mogilevich and Suleiman Kerimov.

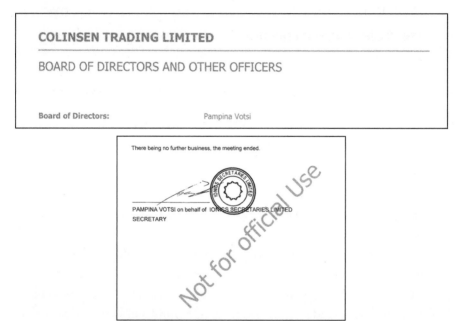

Pampina Votsi represented Colinsen in official legal documents

Mogilevich has been dubbed, "The Most Dangerous Mobster In The World of Organized Crime." In 2009, the FBI placed him on the Top Ten Most Wanted list for more than forty counts of contract murder, racketeering, wire fraud, mail fraud, money laundering, and other economic crimes.

In 2013, it was reported that Mogilevich used the Cyprus company Barlow Investing Limited to hide some of his potentially illegally obtained money. The International Consortium of Investigative Journalists found that Pampina Votsi was one of three Directors for the company.

Another high-profile Russian who hid his money in Cyprus with the help of Vassiliades was businessman and politician Suleiman Kerimov. Pampina Votsi was again listed as a Director of Kerimov's construction and real estate group before he sold his share in the company for $600 million in 2013.

Kerimov was arrested in France in November, 2017 for alleged large-scale tax fraud and money laundering. Vladimir Putin's spokesman, Dmitry Peskov, told reporters in November that Russia "will do everything in our power to protect his lawful interests." The Kremlin has increasingly pressured the French government to release Kerimov, and Russian lawyers have flown to France to attempt to settle the charges.

In a direct connection to the June 2016 Trump Tower meeting, Kerimov is a close associate of Rinat Akhmetshin, the Russian lobbyist and ex-Soviet military intelligence officer who attended the meeting. Akhmetshin worked for Kerimov in 2011 when it was alleged he was involved in the hacking of one of Kerimov's political opponents. Akhmetshin has said in court papers that he coordinated with Kerimov's team to attempt to infiltrate the politician's computer.

Earlier this year, Congress attempted to obtain information about Trump's business interests from Bank of Cyprus Vice Chairman Wilbur Ross, Trump's then-nominee for Secretary of Commerce. Members of Congress sent letters to Ross, but did not receive answers to their questions before his nomination was confirmed. Ross told Senator Bill Nelson at the time that the White House had blocked him from submitting his written responses, but that "he knows of no loans or interaction between the bank or anyone affiliated with the Trump campaign or organization."

Vassiliades and Ross were both prominently involved with Bank of Cyprus during the time the Trump Tower Moscow LOI was in play. Three weeks after the LOI was signed, Sberbank issued a loan to IC Expert in exchange for a pledge of 100% equity from each of the three offshore owners.

These findings raise new questions about what Michael Cohen, Felix Sater, Donald Trump, and Wilbur Ross knew about IC Expert's true ownership, and whether any financial transactions occurred between the parties.

Continuing my research into Mr. Vassiliades unexpectedly brought me to the other side of the globe, in Panama, where Mr. Trump's real estate empire once again connected to Mr. Vassiliades and money-laundering allegations.

Much had been previously written about Trump Ocean Club in Panama and its ties to various criminal elements. A joint *NBC News/Reuters* investigation concluded that "the project was riddled with brokers, customers and investors who have been linked to drug trafficking and international crime." Most of these criminals were associated with the Russian mafia, per Alexandre Ventura, a Brazilian real estate salesman who sold hundreds of units at the Trump Panama hotel and condo and who is now a fugitive after fleeing the country while on bail for real estate fraud charges.

In an effort to continue to investigate Mr. Trump's various real estate dealings around the world, I set off to dig into the major players behind the Panama complex. A global law firm by the name of Alemán, Cordero, Galindo & Lee (Alcogal for short) kept reappearing in my research. The law firm had claimed that they worked alongside the Trump Organization at every step of the way, and acted as the registered agent for many LLCs that purchased units at Trump Panama.

I thought my research into Trump Tower Moscow was complete until I stumbled upon the fact that Alcogal's website listed a Cypriot address with which I was all-too-familiar—the law office of Christodoulos Vassiliades. The address for the Cypriot branch of Alcogal was Vasslaw, the namesake law office of Mr. Vassiliades.

Once again, I found myself digging through the Cyprus business registry to uncover the full relationship between Mr. Vassiliades and Alcogal. By reading through the financial documents for the joint Alcogal-Vassiliades company, called Apex International, it was uncovered that not only did Mr. Vassiliades manage the Cypriot branch of Alcogal, but he was also in charge of the entire financial trust for the Panamanian-based law firm.

The newfound connections between Alcogal and Mr. Vassiliades—and thus Trump Panama and Trump Tower Moscow—completed a multi-national web of money laundering and financial crimes with one common denominator: the Trump Organization.

———

January 12, 2018
Exclusive: Trump's 2015 Deal In Moscow Is Directly Tied to His Ocean Club Hotel in Panama

Law firms in Cyprus and Panama—both with links to allegations of money laundering—connect Trump, his Moscow developer, and his Panama Hotel

Newly obtained documents and open-source information have revealed that Trump's Ocean Club Hotel in Panama and the 2015 Trump Tower Moscow Letter-Of-Intent with Russian developer IC Expert both trace back to the same Cypriot lawyer, Christodoulos Vassiliades.

The shared connection is through Trump's Panamanian law firm, Alemán, Cordero, Galindo & Lee, or Alcogal for short. According to their investor relations brochure, Alcogal "advised the Trump Organization in connection with all matters associated with the acquisition of a casino and the operation of a hotel in Panama". Alcogal can also be found as the registered agent for several anonymous LLCs that own condo units in Trump's Ocean Club. On their website, Alcogal is described as an international law firm based in Panama with offices around the world. The firm's co-founder, Jaime Aleman, is part of a well-connected family and once served as the ambassador to the United States under former President Ricardo Martinelli.

Aleman's Cyprus office address has now been matched to the address for the law firm Christodoulos G. Vassiliades & Co. LLC, owned by its namesake Vassiliades. This is the same Cypriot lawyer who our reporting has revealed owns at least 60% of IC Expert, the Russian developer Donald Trump signed a letter-of-intent with in October 2015. Further, the financial trust for the Panamanian law firm is managed by Vassiliades through the Cyprus-based company Apex International. Vassiliades's company Ionics Nominees serves as a director and secretary for the LLC, meaning Vassiliades has the power to oversee all of the firm's assets. Official documents show that in 2014, Apex International received at least $4.2 million in dividends.

The connection between Vassiliades and Aleman doesn't end there—it ties directly to the Trump Tower Moscow deal. As previously reported in our series about the 2015 LOI, IC Expert Chairman Andrey Rozov falsely certified that he owned 100% of IC Expert when he signed the agreement. Our reporting found that IC Expert is in fact owned by two companies in Cyprus and one in the Marshall Islands. The Cyprus company with a 60% stake, Colinsen Trading Limited, is owned by Vassiliades through the same Ionic Nominees that manages Alcogal's trust. New documents now show that the company with a 15% stake, Capilana Trading Limited, traces to the British Virgin Islands and is registered to Alcogal.

ALLEGATIONS OF MONEY LAUNDERING

This newfound connection between Trump, IC Expert, Vassiliades, and Alcogal adds to a multi-country web of various financial crimes including fraud and money laundering.

As detailed in our previous reporting, Christodoulos Vassiliades is a prominent lawyer who owns an international law firm based in Cyprus. After the 2013 crash that nearly wiped out the Bank of Cyprus, Vassiliades was personally nominated by the Bank of Moscow to assume an 8.37% proxy share of the bank. The share represented, at least in part, the amount Vassiliades's anonymous Russian clients had deposited in the bank. A source familiar with Cyprus's banking system said that Vassiliades primarily functions as an "introducer" between wealthy Russians and Ukrainians and the Bank.

Panicos Demetriades, former Governor of the Central Bank of Cyprus, and author of *A Diary of the Euro Crisis in Cyprus: Lessons for Bank Recovery and Resolution*—a book that explains how politically connected law firms facilitated financial flows between Russia and Cyprus—confirmed that Vassiliades was one of the most influential law firms in the country.

Vassiliades has been connected to money laundering and embezzlement schemes involving oligarchs and businessmen from multiple countries—largely through his company Ionics Nominees. Vassiliades, who serves as the honorary consul to Belize and has in the past worked for the law firm owned by the President of Cyprus, is connected to these allegations of financial crimes by way of the anonymous LLCs he sets up for clients. The three most prominent allegations of money laundering and embezzlement come from Ukraine, Austria, and Romania. These three cases all allege that Ionics Nominees Limited helped wash money illegally obtained by businessmen and politicians.

Mokas, The Unit for Combating Money Laundering in Cyprus, said they were aware of reports tying Vassiliades to these crimes. However, they stressed that Vassiliades "is not and never has been under investigation." After providing additional details proving that Vassiliades owns Ionics Nominees Limited, Mokas said, "This office does not intend to continue correspondence with you on this matter."

Alcogal has been mired in money-laundering investigations of their own. An investigation found that introducers contracting with BSI bank in Switzerland used Alcogal to move money out of the UK and into offshores through a series of shell companies. Alcogal was fined in 2015 for failing to review and keep up to date customer due-diligence information. Apart from this fine, Alcogal has been connected to numerous money laundering schemes. An ICIJ report in 2016 found that Alcogal set up at least five companies that were used by Augusto Pinochet, Chile's former dictator. A Panama Papers report declared Alcogal, "an infamous Panamanian offshore provider that has . . . aided in the laundering of money for well-known criminals."

TROUBLE IN PARADISE

Allegations of money laundering and other scandals associated with Trump's Panama Ocean Club have been well-documented and reported on. However, the link between Trump's law firm in Panama, the Ocean Club hotel, and the 2015 Moscow deal has never been made until now. The implications of the deal are better understood when evaluated within the context of Trump's fledgling presidential bid.

Trump's management company was fired by the Condo Board in Panama just one month into a campaign that Trump repeatedly claimed would be "self-funded." Angry condo owners accused the Trump-installed team of mismanagement, misuse of funds, and a refusal to share financial records.

At the time, the Ocean Club hotel was by far Trump's most lucrative international licensing and management deal. Reports of Trump's earnings have been estimated between $32 and $50 million since the deal was inked in 2006 and doors opened in 2011. In Trump's 2015 financial disclosures, which have never been independently verified, Trump claimed earnings of at least $5.8M over the previous eighteen months. One of his Panama companies claimed "$5M and above" in the document, meaning the true amount could really be anything.

While it is unclear how the firing affected Trump's access to bank accounts and payments from the hotel at the time, what is clear is that Trump did not intend to walk away from the forty-year lease without a fight. An AP exclusive in November 2015 revealed that Trump had secretly filed a $75 million lawsuit against both condo owners and the developer.

We now know that at this same point in the campaign, work on the Trump Tower Moscow deal was already underway with a company owned by the same Cypriot lawyer who managed the trust and provided the Cyprus office address for Trump's Panamanian law firm. As Michael Cohen has disclosed, the Trump Organization had already gotten to work picking out architects and designers, while Cohen himself was involved with financing discussions.

Earlier this year we learned that despite the July 2015 firing, the settlement of Trump's lawsuit eventually allowed his company to retain management of the hotel. In Trump's 2016 financial filings, he declared earnings of $6.8 million from the hotel. According to a press release from the Ocean Club sales agency, condo units that had remained unsold for years sold out completely during the 2015–2016 campaign season.

Given these revelations connecting Trump's Moscow Deal to his existing business in Panama, it grows increasingly less credible that the deal would have fallen through for the reasons Michael Cohen publicly alleged—because he had "lost confidence [IC Expert] would be able to obtain the real estate, financing and government approvals necessary to bring the proposal to fruition." Coupled with our exclusive reporting that shows that IC Expert received a loan of at least $162M from Sberbank three weeks after the LOI was signed, and that amnesty for negligent homicide was granted by the government to Chairman Andrey Rozov, Cohen's statements appear misleading.

Congress must release the testimony from Michael Cohen. Given the breadth of knowledge gained from the Fusion GPS testimony, it is likely that Cohen's testimony includes details that deserve to be seen by the public.

————

During my months of research into Trump Tower Moscow, I kept returning to a basic yet increasingly abstruse question: Who was the real owner of IC Expert?

I knew that IC Expert was officially owned by three offshore LLCs in Cyprus, the Marshall Islands, and the British Virgin Islands. The Cyprus LLC ended up with an uncooperative nominal owner—Mr. Vassiliades. The laws of the Marshall Islands are so strict that the only public information about companies is their names and identification numbers; a dead end. The British Virgin Islands LLC, though, I posited, could possibly be investigated enough to shed light on who owns that slice of IC Expert.

When filing documents in the British Virgin Islands, a company can choose to hide the filing from any public records or requests, a decision that the vast majority of companies choose to make. Cyprus, however, as we previously learned from the analysis of Mr. Vassiliades, has no such privacy option.

As of early 2016, the ownership structure of IC Expert was the following.

1. Colinsen Trading Limited (Cyprus), owns 60%
2. Trianguli Limited (the Marshall Islands), owns 25%
3. Ecoprestizh (Russia) -> Carnberg Development Limited (Cyprus) -> Capilana Trading Limited (the British Virgin Islands), owns 15%.

The trail of that third LLC offered some opportunities to gather more information. The business records I acquired for Carnberg

Development Limited included minutes from a meeting of the Board of Directors. Present at the meeting was a representative of Capilana Trading Limited, the owner of Carnberg Development Limited and thus the owner of 15% of IC Expert.

Ioanna Theofilou, a Cypriot national, affirmed in these audited documents that she was the sole shareholder of Capilana Trading Limited. Like Mr. Vassiliades, Ms. Theofilou was clearly acting as a nominal owner to mask the true identity of the owner of Capilana Trading Limited.

I raked through Ms. Theofilou's business record, and at nearly every company in which Ms. Theofilou worked, there was one beneficial owner—one of the most powerful Russian oligarchs, politically and financially: Oleg Deripaska.

February 9, 2018
Newly Discovered Evidence Suggests Oleg Deripaska May Own Part of Trump's Chosen Moscow Developer

Deripaska's offshore manager revealed as the sole shareholder of a company that owns part of Trump's Moscow developer

Newly discovered financial documents and ownership history records suggest that the Kremlin-connected oligarch Oleg Deripaska may own part of the development company with which Donald Trump signed a Letter of Intent (LOI) in late 2015 to build Trump Tower Moscow.

The agreement was signed by Donald Trump on October 28th, 2015, four months into his presidential run. Presented by Felix Sater, the Letter of Intent confirmed a non-binding agreement between Trump Acquisition LLC and the Russian development company IC Expert. According to Michael Cohen, the deal was abandoned in January 2016 because he "lost confidence that the prospective licensee would be able to obtain the real estate, financing and government approvals." Previous exclusive reporting has shown that the Russian

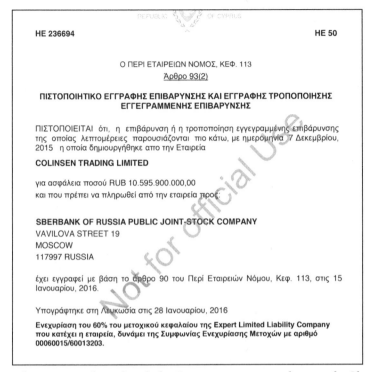

Financial transaction logged with the Cyprus government showing the Sberbank loan to Colinsen Trading Limited, IC Expert's main shareholder

state-owned Sberbank issued a loan worth approximately $162 million to IC Expert three weeks after the LOI was signed.

Capilana Trading Limited in the British Virgin Islands was the majority owner until just months before Donald Trump partnered with IC Expert, when Capilana's share in the Russian development company dropped to 15%. Weeks after IC Expert's chairman Andrey Rozov was granted amnesty by the Russian government in a negligent homicide case, the majority ownership of IC Expert was transferred to a prominent Cyprus lawyer in order to mask the true ownership.

Deripaska's connection to Capilana is through his Cypriot manager—Ioanna Theofilou. Whereas many Cypriot directors and secretaries act for hundreds or thousands of companies, Theofilou is only involved with a few dozen, with the plurality of those being companies owned by Deripaska. For example, subsidiaries of Deripaska's largest companies, En+ and RUSAL, list Theofilou as their director and secretary. When

Deripaska established a Panamanian company under the RUSAL umbrella, he again entrusted Theofilou to be one of his only directors. The only other Panamanian company in which Theofilou is a director cannot immediately be traced to Deripaska, though the same officers are involved, and the incorporation dates are only one year apart.

British Virgin Islands law allows the principals of a company to remain anonymous. This secrecy makes it an attractive destination for high-profile businesspeople to register their companies. Normally, this would be the end of the trail for a company such as Capilana, but when conducting business in a foreign country such as Cyprus, principals of a company must be present.

Exclusively obtained 2014 financial documents in Cyprus left a hint: Ioanna Theofilou was the sole shareholder of Capilana

PRESENT: IOANNA THEOFILOU on behalf of CAPILANA TRADING LTD	Chryso Argyrou. Date 3 1 JAN 2017 -SOLE SHAREHOLDER The Registrar

Documents submitted to the British Virgin Islands government indicate that the only changes to the directors of Capilana occurred in late 2016, months after the Letter of Intent was signed. It cannot be confirmed that Theofilou is acting on behalf of Deripaska in this instance, though a good portion of her work in the past decade has been for the Russian oligarch's most prized companies. The shareholder of the company has never been altered.

Previously, it was established that two of Deripaska's CEOs, Stalbek Mishakov and Pavel Lebedev, were in charge of IC Expert's sister company Expert Development. One of Deripaska's closest associates and one-time personal lawyer, Mishakov served as CEO of Expert Development for over a year, and oversaw the development of a large shopping center in Reutov, Moscow. At the same time he was serving as CEO of Expert Development, Mishakov was also part of the leadership team at En+ Group, an energy company controlled by Deripaska. The multi-billion dollar conglomerate is one of Deripaska's most successful ventures to date.

Lebedev and Mishakov previously worked together at another Deripaska-owned company, Altius Development, which built the Olympic Village for

S.No	Previous Name	Foreign Character Name	Date Range or Cease Date	
			From	To
1	CAPILANA TRADING Ltd.		15/08/2008	

Transaction History

S.No	Date	Transaction Number	Description	Status	Eforms/Attachments
1	15/08/2008	T080590089	Application for Incorporation (BC)	Approved	Application for Incorporation (BC) Memorandum and Articles of the Company
2	15/08/2008	T080589614	Name Reservation (10 days)	Approved	Name Reservation (10 days)
3	04/09/2009	T090509671	Annual Fee Submission (BC)	Approved	Annual Submission
4	06/04/2010	T100153242	Request for Certificate of Goodstanding	Approved	Request for Certificate of Good Standing
5	19/07/2010	T100476801	Request for Certificate of Goodstanding	Approved	Request for Certificate of Good Standing
6	22/07/2010	T100483511	Annual Fee Submission (BC)	Approved	Annual Submission
7	20/09/2010	T100574508	Request for Certificate of Goodstanding	Approved	Request for Certificate of Good Standing
8	29/09/2011	T110639485	Annual Fee Submission (BC)	Approved	Annual Submission
9	11/06/2013	T130453017	Annual Fee Submission (BC)	Approved	Annual Submission
10	11/06/2013	T130453021	Request for Certificate of Goodstanding	Approved	Request for Certificate of Good Standing
11	14/11/2014	T140788346	Annual Fee Submission (BC)	Approved	Annual Submission
12	03/12/2014	T140909465	Notice of Change of Registered Agent	Approved	Notice of Change of Registered Agent
13	23/12/2014	T140946537	Amendments of Memorandum and / Or Articles of Association	Approved	Amendments Of Memorandum And Or Articles Of Association
					The attachment restated memorandum/articles incorporates the amendment made
14	24/11/2015	T150845488	Annual Fee Submission (BC)	Approved	Annual Submission
15	29/08/2016	T160599987	Register of Members or Directors	Approved	Register of Directors
16	22/11/2016	T161045305	Annual Fee Submission (BC)	Approved	Annual Submission
17	07/12/2016	T170016167	Notice of Change of Registered Office Address	Approved	Notice Change Of Registered Office Address
18	07/03/2017	T170378258	Request for Certificate of Goodstanding	Approved	Request for Certificate of Good Standing
19	14/03/2017	T170406576	Notice of Filing of Restated Memorandum and Articles of Association	Approved	Notice Of Filing Of Restated Memorandum And Articles Of Association
					The attachment restated memorandum/articles incorporates the amendment made

the 2014 Winter Olympics. Mishakov, Lebedev, and Andrey Rozov also all served on the Board of Directors of the industrial firm 1MPZ.

Deripaska has become a key player in the investigation into Russian interference in the 2016 US elections. Former Trump campaign manager Paul Manafort was deeply in debt to Deripaska, at one point asking how he can use his position on the Trump team to "get whole". In July 2016, Manafort offered to give Deripaska private briefings about the campaign. Press officers for Deripaska did not immediately respond to requests for comment.

The revelations come as Russian opposition leader Alexey Navalny released a video showing Deripaska and Russian Deputy Prime Minister Sergei Prikhodko secretly meeting on a yacht in Norway in August 2016. The meeting came days after Manafort had dinner with his longtime employee with suspected ties to Russian intelligence, Konstantin Kilimnik. Kilimnik acted as an intermediary throughout the campaign for Manafort to reach Deripaska.

Manafort did not join the Trump team until late February 2016, approximately one month after Michael Cohen claims the Moscow deal was terminated. The potential of Deripaska having a share in Trump's Moscow developer raises new questions about when the Russian oligarch first may have had contact with the Trump campaign.

January 25, 2019
The Moscow Project and the Missing Six Billion Rubles

The developer of the proposed Trump Tower in Moscow that was negotiating with Michael Cohen and the Trump Organization appears to have an unaccounted six billion rubles, or $90,000,000, after it received a loan from Sberbank in the weeks following the agreement with Trump.

Exclusively obtained company documents show a massive discrepancy between the purported amount of the loan and the actual amount of capital that Sberbank extended to IC Expert, the developer.

At the time of the Letter-of-Intent agreement with the Trump Organization, IC Expert had one other major development underway in the Moscow suburb of Reutov—a massive residential development complex called Novokosino-2. The microdistrict also includes public facilities such as schools, parks, and shopping centers. In an effort to fund the construction of two of the seventeen buildings in the complex, IC Expert reached a line-of-credit agreement with the state-owned Sberbank.

The loan agreement was first realized on November 18, 2015, just three weeks after Trump signed the Letter-of-Intent with IC Expert's chairman Andrey Rozov. In December 2015, three offshore companies that comprised the ownership of IC Expert pledged 100% of their share capital to

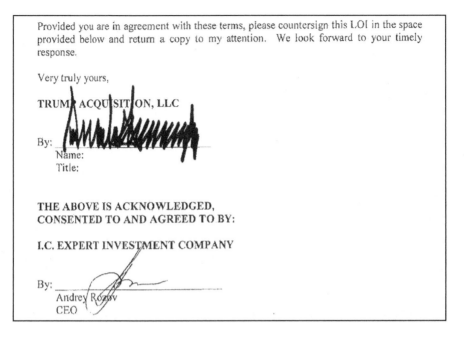

Provided you are in agreement with these terms, please countersign this LOI in the space provided below and return a copy to my attention. We look forward to your timely response.

Very truly yours,

TRUMP ACQUISITION, LLC

By: _____
    Name:
    Title:

**THE ABOVE IS ACKNOWLEDGED,
CONSENTED TO AND AGREED TO BY:**

I.C. EXPERT INVESTMENT COMPANY

By: _____
    Andrey Rozov
    CEO

begin executing the loan, and money began flowing from Sberbank to IC Expert.

The true owners of the three shell companies remain unknown, though at least two of those companies (comprising 75% of the shares) were controlled by a Cypriot lawyer known for his ties to Russian elite and involvement in multiple money laundering schemes. The lawyer, Christodoulos Vassiliades, is also a Director for Sberbank's Cyprus branch—raising questions about a possible conflict of interest in this case.

According to business documents in the project declaration for the two Novokosino-2 buildings (numbers sixteen and seventeen), Sberbank provided 4,595,900,000 (4.595 billion) rubles to fund the majority of the construction. The declarations for buildings sixteen and seventeen from IC Expert note the Sberbank loan.

The purpose and amount of the Sberbank line-of-credit was affirmed in news reports and at least one independent analysis of IC Expert's finances.

The Novokosino-2 project, and in particular buildings sixteen and seventeen, were the subject of dozens of lawsuits from angry prospective homeowners. The construction on the buildings was delayed multiple times, and as a result, many homebuyers lost their money. According to one

Russian news article, building sixteen was finished in 2018 while building seventeen remains under construction. Two sources familiar with the matter said that bankruptcy proceedings had begun against IC Expert, though that could not be independently verified.

The project outlines for buildings sixteen and seventeen noting the Sberbank loan differ greatly from the true amount of the line of credit, per official, audited Cypriot corporate documents. The real value of the Sberbank loan, as seen below, was 10.595 billion rubles—precisely 6 billion rubles more than IC Expert had claimed.

Ποσό που διασφαλίστηκε με την Επιβάρυνση	Μέχρι και το ποσό των 10,595,900,000.00 Ρουβλιών (δέκα δισεκατομμύρια πεντακόσια ενενήντα πέντε εκατομμύρια εννιακόσιες χιλιάδες ρούβλια) που οφείλονται από την Expert LLC στην Sberbank δυνάμει της Συμφωνίας Πίστωσης.
	Up to the amount of 10,595,900,000.00 RUB (ten billion five hundred ninety five million nine hundred thousand rubles) owed by Expert LLC to Sberbank pursuant to the Credit Line Agreement.

A second document filed with the Cypriot government confirmed that IC Expert (via the Cypriot offshore company which was majority owner of the Russian firm) owed Sberbank the full 10.595 billion rubles, indicating that the entire line-of-credit was executed.

The inconsistency between the stated amount of the loan and the actual amount of money available to IC Expert from Sberbank has not been previously reported. In response to a request for comment, the Press Office of Sberbank issued the following statement:

> Sberbank has to ensure the confidentiality of its clients' banking secrets and therefore cannot comment on any of the banking operations that clients perform.

Though there is no public evidence that any money flowed between any Trump associates and IC Expert, a letter from IC Expert CEO Andrey Rozov to Trump's lawyer Michael Cohen in September 2015 revealed a plan to use a company in the United States to handle any matters relating to Trump Tower Moscow. Felix Sater, a Trump associate and convicted Russian mob-connected fraudster turned FBI informant, acted as an intermediary between Cohen and Rozov and other Russians throughout the Trump Tower Moscow negotiations.

"For our potential joint-venture contract we will use a U.S. corporation"
—Andrey Rozov to Michael Cohen in September 2015

It is unclear if such a corporation was ever incorporated in the United States. Requests for comment to IC Expert and a lawyer for Felix Sater went unanswered. Peter Carr, a Spokesman for Robert Mueller's office, declined to comment on their ongoing investigation.

Separately, it has been revealed, via the same letter from Rozov to Cohen, that Andrey Rozov was behind the purchase and quick sale of a Manhattan office building in 2015.

"I also own a 12 story office building in Manhattan at 22 West 38th Street, which I acquired last year . . ."

The sale, which was first reported by independent journalist Wendy Siegelman when the buyer of the office building was unknown, saw Rozov turn an $8.1M profit just months after an all-cash purchase of the building for $35.5M. Three LLCs controlled by New York City real estate investment and management firm Dalan Management and real estate developer David Karmi made the 2015 purchase from Rozov, according to New York State property documents.

IN WITNESS WHEREOF, the party of the first part has duly executed this deed the date first above written.

22 WEST 38TH STREET ASSOCIATES, LLC

By: _____
Felix Sater
Authorized Signatory

Sater represented Rozov in the sale in December 2015, just as the two were in discussions about Trump Tower Moscow with the Trump Organization.

Congressional investigators plan on scrutinizing the attempt to build Trump Tower Moscow during the 2016 campaign.

"[The House Intelligence Committee] is already working to secure additional witness testimony and documents related to the Trump Tower Moscow deal and other investigative matters," Chairman Adam Schiff said in an interview with CNBC in mid-January.

"Our Committee is determined to get to the bottom of this and follow the evidence wherever it may lead."

Subsequent Information

In late November 2018, Mr. Cohen pleaded guilty to lying to Congress regarding his testimony on the Trump Tower Moscow negotiations during 2015 and 2016. Among other things, Mr. Cohen admitted that he lied to Congressional investigators when he said that the negotiations regarding Trump Tower Moscow ended in January of 2016, instead admitting to Mr. Mueller that the *BuzzFeed* reports were accurate and the project remained active until at least June.

According to his guilty plea, Cohen also kept Mr. Trump and other Trump family members, mainly Don Jr. and Ivanka, informed about the project. Cohen, "discussed the status and progress of the Moscow Project with [Trump] on more than the three occasions COHEN claimed to the Committee, and he briefed family members of [Trump] within the Company about the project.

Mr. Cohen also held a substantive phone conversation with one of Mr. Peskov's close aides, per the court documents. Previously, Mr. Cohen had maintained that he sent an email to a general email address for Mr. Peskov and never received a response. The charging documents proved that Mr. Cohen did indeed receive a response from Mr. Peskov's office and that the two discussed the details of Trump Tower Moscow.

The full extent of Mr. Cohen's efforts to build Trump Tower Moscow in 2016, including with whom in Moscow he spoke, remain to be uncovered. The question of who on the Moscow side of these negotiations spoke with Mr. Cohen and others in the Trump Organization about this deal remains a critical question for investigators.

Hours after the guilty plea was announced, *BuzzFeed* published a new report on Trump Tower Moscow stating that Mr. Sater and Mr. Cohen planned to offer Mr. Putin a $50 million penthouse in the proposed tower. "This sure looks like a bribe of a foreign official — a violation of the Foreign Corrupt Practices Act that could subject those involved to criminal liability," said Texas Congressman Joaquin Castro, member of the House Intelligence Committee.

According to the tremendous reporting of Anthony Cormier and Jason Leopold, two FBI agents told them that Mr. Cohen "was in frequent contact with foreign individuals about the real estate venture — and that some of these individuals had knowledge of or played a role in 2016 election meddling. The identity of those individuals remains unknown."

Needless to say, if this contact is confirmed, the significance of the Trump Tower Moscow negotiations increases monumentally. The deal would morph from a potential shady business deal with multiple instances of criminal liability for those close to Mr. Trump, to a direct line of communication from the Trump campaign to the Russian forces that were involved in the cyber warfare conducted against Mr. Trump's political opponents.

Abstract

The Trump Organization's discussions with Russian nationals and government officials to build Trump Tower Moscow during the 2015-2016 election signifies some of the clearest evidence of a wide-ranging conspiracy between the campaign and Russian officials. For Mr. Trump, the endgame of having his name atop the tallest building in Europe would have satisfied a lifelong professional dream of his. For Mr. Putin and the Russian government, the negotiations provided more than enough material to blackmail the eventual President of the United States and create a situation in which they had control over Mr. Trump and his foreign policy decisions. By lying about the details of the Trump Tower Moscow talks, Mr. Cohen and Mr. Trump gave the Kremlin an incredible amount of power to hold over their heads.

As my reporting has shown, the Russian government was involved in the process of a potential Trump Tower Moscow deal since before Mr. Trump even announced his candidacy. The development company that was slated to build the tower was structured in such a way that the Trump Organization had absolutely no idea with whom it was doing business. The involvement of a Cypriot lawyer who has numerous connections to money laundering schemes made this deal a trifecta of crimson red flags that Mr. Trump failed to heed.

The moment Mr. Trump signed the letter-of-intent to build Trump Tower Moscow on October 28, 2015, his organization and his campaign for president were compromised by a foreign adversary. The subsequent lies by everyone involved only furthered the Kremlin's power to influence the policy of the Trump administration. They knew that Mr. Cohen, Mr. Trump and others were not only involved in shady business negotiations in 2015 and 2016, but also lying about these negotiations.

The Russian government had enormous leverage over the Trump White House the day that Mr. Trump was sworn into office, and everyone involved in the Trump Tower Moscow deal knew it.

The Secret 2016 Manhattan Meetings

Who's Who:
- **Donald Trump Jr.:** Son of Donald Trump. Close political adviser in 2015 and 2016. Executive Vice President of the Trump Organization.
- **Jared Kushner:** Son-in-law of Donald Trump. Acted as one of the lead decision-makers in Mr. Trump's campaign.
- **Paul Manafort:** Mr. Trump's longtime friend and Campaign Chairman in the Summer of 2016.
- **Aras Agalarov:** Azerbaijani-Russian billionaire close to President Putin.
- **Emin Agalarov:** Son of Aras Agalarov. Close friend of the Trump family since 2013.
- **Natalia Veselnitskaya:** Russian attorney connected to military intelligence and top Kremlin officials.
- **Ike Kaveladze:** The Agalarov's Vice President and right-hand businessman.

Overview

Much has been made of the now-infamous 2016 Trump Tower meeting with Donald Trump Jr., Jared Kushner, Paul Manafort, and well-connected Russians who promised dirt on Hillary Clinton. The June 9th meeting remains at the heart of the investigation into possible collusion between the Trump campaign and the Russian government. Though the meeting itself should not be overlooked, the events preceding and succeeding the rendezvous are far more significant.

Originating from a meeting between Russia's Prosecutor General (the equivalent to the United States Attorney General) and the billionaire Azerbaijani-Russian real estate developer Aras Agalarov, the request to meet with the Trump campaign came from Rob Goldstone, a publicist for the son of Mr. Agalarov, Emin.

Mr. Goldstone wrote, "The Crown prosecutor of Russia met with [Emin's] father Aras this morning and in their meeting offered to provide the Trump campaign with some official documents and information that would incriminate Hillary." Goldstone continued, "[t]his is obviously very high level and sensitive information but is part of Russia and its government's support for Mr. Trump - helped along by Aras and Emin."

In the months following the disclosure of his role in setting up the meeting, Mr. Goldstone has denied that his email was referring to Yuri Chaika, the Russian Prosecutor General. "I was never referring to Russia's prosecutor general oh [sic] my email - but to Natalia Veselnitskaya," Goldstone tweeted in December 2018.

Several data points cast doubt on Mr. Goldstone's claims, however. Most importantly, a memo that Ms. Veselnitskaya brought to the Trump Tower meeting contained many of the exact same talking points as a memo circulated by Mr. Chaika just weeks earlier. The Veselnitskaya document was, at some points, verbatim to the Chaika memo. Additionally, Mr. Goldstone's exact wording in the email was "the Crown prosecutor"—a hint that he was referring to the top prosecutor in the country, Mr. Chaika. Mr. Goldstone himself recognizes this apparent discrepancy, suggesting that the use of "the" instead of "a" was merely a typo.

Whatever the case, Donald Trump Jr. notoriously responded to Mr. Goldstone's email, enthusiastically stating, "if it's what you say I love it especially later in the summer."

It is illegal to accept any monetary donation or anything of value from a foreign entity during the course of an election.

By definitively stating, in writing, "I love it" to the Russian government overture, Donald Trump Jr. attempted to enter into a criminal conspiracy with the Russian government. It was made clear that the Russian government wanted to help Mr. Trump's campaign by passing along opposition research obtained on Mrs. Clinton, and Mr. Trump Jr. responded affirmatively.

Receiving this response from the upper echelon of the Trump campaign amounted to a coup for the Russian government. They now had compromising material on those closest to Mr. Trump—his son, son-in-law, and campaign chairman. Imagine this headline during the final weeks of the 2016: "Trump Inner Circle Took Meeting Set Up by Russian Government in Effort to Obtain Dirt on Hillary Clinton." Such a headline would have been devastating for Mr. Trump's chances at winning the presidency.

It is no surprise then, that the Republican candidate for president made official moves favorable to Russia, including removing a provision in the GOP platform that called for arming the Ukrainian government in its ongoing war against Russian forces. Mr. Trump continued to praise President Putin effusively as Mr. Putin's government waged a cyber war against Mr. Trump's political rivals.

It is also no surprise that the ex-British spy Christopher Steele, who was compiling the Trump dossier, said in July 2016 that Russian intelligence believed that they had Donald Trump "over a barrel".

What ended up happening at the meeting, where by all accounts the Russians did not end up bringing dirt on Mrs. Clinton, pales in comparison to the significance of the emails preceding the event.

The relationship between the Agalarov family and the Trump inner circle dates back to three years prior to the Trump Tower meeting.

To fully understand the now-infamous 2016 Trump Tower meeting with the Russian lawyer and senior members of the Trump campaign, one must become familiar with a much-different meeting that took place three years earlier. Prior to announcing that Miss Universe 2013 would be held in Moscow, Mr. Trump joined a private dinner at a steakhouse located in the Palazzo resort. Among the attendees were Mr. Trump's Russian partners for the pageant, Aras and Emin Agalarov, as well as members of the Trump inner circle, longtime lawyer Michael Cohen, bodyguard Keith Schiller, and others. The November pageant was to be held at the Crocus City Hall in Moscow, owned by Mr. Agalarov's conglomerate of Crocus companies.

It was during this late-2013 trip to Moscow that the ex-British spy

Christopher Steele would later report that Russian intelligence secretly recorded Mr. Trump engaging in lewd acts with prostitutes. Mr. Steele had multiple sources tell him that during Mr. Trump's trips to Russia, starting in the 1980s and concluding with the 2013 pageant, Mr. Trump engaged in deviant sexual behavior that the Russian government could hold over him as blackmail.

Two sources, Mr. Steele wrote, "believe Azeri business associate of Trump, [Aras] Agalarov will know the details."

To fully understand the repercussions of the 2016 Trump Tower meeting, one must have a clear view of everyone that attended: Donald Trump Jr, Paul Manafort, Jared Kushner, the Russian lawyer Natalia Veselnitskaya, her translator Anatoli Samochornov, her associate Rinat Akhmetshin, Robert Goldstone, the Agalarov's publicist, and Ike Kaveladze, the Vice President of Crocus and representative of the Agalarovs.

The official narrative is that Mr. Trump had no knowledge of the meeting and was not told of the meeting until it was reported in the press. It turns out, however, that Mr. Trump knew not only the three Americans in the meeting, but also two of the other attendees. Exclusively reported pictures and documentation of the summer-2013 Las Vegas meeting established that Mr. Trump knew most of the people in the room during the 2016 Trump Tower meeting. This documentation was the basis of my first report on the Trump Tower meeting.

Also occurring around the time of the Trump Tower meeting was a series of suspicious money transfers made by Mr. Agalarov, who had recently been told by the Russian Prosecutor General that the Russian government had dirt on Hillary Clinton. Mr. Agalarov moved tens of millions of dollars from bank accounts in the British Virgin Islands to accounts in the United States, as first reported by *BuzzFeed News*. In fact, days before the Trump Tower meeting, Mr. Agalarov sent what would add up to over $1.2M to companies controlled by Mr. Kaveladze in the United States. The men claim that the transfers were for legitimate business purposes.

The banks utilized by Mr. Agalarov and Mr. Kaveladze marked some of the transfers as suspicious, as the transactions appeared to have no legitimate purpose. They didn't fit the normal pattern of business transactions by Mr. Agalarov, and the money was quickly moved to other accounts, a red flag for major banking institutions. Mr. Mueller has taken an avid interest in these money transfers that occurred in the days leading up to, and following, the Trump Tower meeting.

What was not uncovered by *BuzzFeed* and other media outlets that reported on the movement of Mr. Agalarov's money was a Delaware shell company that he incorporated just weeks before the infamous meeting. A comprehensive look at this company revealed links to money-laundering schemes and a New York-based tax attorney with shady clients. This company was the basis of my second report on the Trump Tower meeting, bylined with the *Guardian* and Jon Swaine.

The Process

As a beginning journalist balancing college with this work, I had limited resources and limited connections. Most of my early investigations relied on already-reported news, such as the Trump Tower meeting, as the starting point for my research. Whereas these big news organizations had to keep up with the rapidly evolving saga and move on to the next story, I took the approach of doing more thorough, deep diving on information that was already public. (As I discussed in more detail in the Preface section of this book.)

After all of the attendees and organizers of the Trump Tower meeting were identified by major media outlets, I started a comprehensive open-source investigation into each person. In a situation like this, Google can be a hell of a tool when utilized properly. For example, searching Emin Agalarov's name in Russian alongside "Trump" returned hundreds of thousands of results, most of them about the recently reported 2016 activities. However, searching "Эмин Агаларов" (Emin Agalarov) and "Трамп" (Trump) and setting the parameters of the search to look for web pages created before 2016 returned a much narrower set of results.

Most of the hits were regarding the 2013 Miss Universe pageant. Refining my search to only include results prior to November 2013 (the month of the pageant) led me to a picture that captured my attention: Mr. Trump, Michael Cohen, Mr. Trump's personal lawyer, and Keith Schiller, Mr. Trump's bodyguard, seated at a dinner table with both Agalarovs, Mr. Goldstone, and others.

The picture was posted on the personal blog of a woman named Yulia Alferova, a Crocus employee and friend of Emin Agalarov. Before I could report my findings, CNN posted a video from the event in question—the 2013 dinner in Las Vegas. However, they left out a major detail: Mr. Kaveladze's attendance was not noted. This photographic proof that Mr. Trump knew Mr. Kaveladze meant that the eventual 2016 candidate for president personally knew five of the eight Trump Tower meeting participants, making it all the more likely that he had at least some knowledge of the June 9, 2016 conference.

––––––––

November 22, 2017
In 2013, Donald Trump Met One of the Russian Attendees to the 2016 Trump Tower Meeting

Ike Kaveladze, an accused money launderer, was a guest at a private dinner hosted by Donald Trump in 2013

The eighth person identified at the infamous Trump Tower meeting in June 2016, Ike Kaveladze, met Donald Trump in Las Vegas in 2013. The private dinner was held at the Trump hotel in Las Vegas on June 17th, 2013. Also in attendance were Emin and Aras Agalarov and Rob Goldstone.

The pictures, discovered on the personal blog of one of the Agalarov's business associates, Yulia Alferova, depict a dinner of no more than twenty people.

The dinner in Trump International Hotel in Las Vegas preceded a press conference in which Trump announced that the upcoming Miss Universe pageant was to be held in Moscow in a complex owned by the Agalarovs.

Kaveladze was identified as the last person who attended the June 2016 Trump Tower meeting in which Donald Trump Jr., Jared Kushner, and Paul Manafort expected to receive "dirt" on Hillary Clinton. Trump Jr claims that the meeting did not yield any opposition research on Clinton, describing the encounter as a "wasted 20 minutes."

Special Counsel Robert Mueller is investigating President Trump for his role in dictating the Trump Jr. response, which was riddled with falsehoods. Trump, Trump Jr., and Kushner maintain that the President was not told that the meeting took place until it was revealed by the *Washington Post* in 2017.

Ike Kaveladze is the Vice President of the Crocus Group owned by Aras Agalarov. He is a Russian national currently living in California. Before Kaveladze joined the Crocus Group, he was locked up in a months-long congressional investigation into Russian money laundering. A *New York Times* article in 2000 outed Kaveladze as a main conspirator in a money laundering scheme involving over $1.4 billion through the use of 2,000 shell companies. Kaveladze and his attorney Scott Balber have described the report as a "Russian witch hunt." Balber did not immediately respond to quest for comment.

The pictures were posted by Yulia Alferova, who helped organize Miss Universe on behalf of the Agalarovs and was seen with Trump numerous times during his stay in Moscow in 2013.

––––––––

Nearly a year later, the Trump Tower meeting was back making headline news as *BuzzFeed News* reported that Mr. Agalarov conducted a series of suspicious money transfers before and after the meeting and inauguration. One of the entities that transferred millions of dollars into the United States was a British Virgin Islands company called Silver Valley Consulting Corporation. Running this name in an open source corporate database revealed companies by the same name set up in Hong Kong, Denmark, and . . . Delaware.

To make sure these were all controlled by Mr. Agalarov, I purchased business documents for the Hong Kong company from the local government. The documents showed Mr. Agalarov as the sole shareholder.

Acquiring documents from Delaware, believe it or not, is much more difficult than most other countries around the world. Without revealing too much, I was able to eventually get in contact with a person who had access to some of these documents in Delaware. To protect my source, I can't say too much more about this step of the process except that the documents I received showed that a New York tax accountant by the name of Ilya Bykov incorporated the company in May 2016. I immediately drafted and sent an email to Mr. Bykov asking who was the beneficial owner of the company and why it was set up.

I awoke the next morning to a voicemail from an unfamiliar voice, "Hello Scott, this is Ilya Bykov," the thick Russian accent said, "You sent me an email, you had a question about Silver Valley Consulting registered in 2016. If you're still interested in this information please give me a call."

To my surprise, I also had a signed letter from Mr. Bykov sent to my email address answering all of my questions and more. He confirmed that Mr. Agalarov was behind the Delaware company, and that it was registered to handle investment opportunities that did not materialize.

While I was digesting this information, I received a message from Jon Swaine, a reporter at the *Guardian* with whom I had previously written an unrelated story: "I had a call from a certain Russian accountant asking me to vouch for you!"

Mr. Bykov had called Mr. Swaine after seeing our names together in a byline for the *Guardian*. Unbeknownst to me, Mr. Swaine already had pages of notes on Mr. Bykov and his connections to other high-profile Russians. We compared our information and realized we had more than enough for a full story on the nexus of Mr. Agalarov, Mr. Bykov, and this shell company registered weeks before the Trump Tower meeting.

October 18, 2018 (byline with the *Guardian*'s Jon Swaine)
Revealed: Russian Billionaire Set Up US Company Before Trump Tower Meeting

Aras Agalarov, who helped arrange the meeting with Donald Trump Jr in June 2016, formed a shell company with an accountant who has had clients accused of money laundering and embezzlement

A Russian billionaire who orchestrated the June 2016 Trump Tower meeting formed a new American shell company a month beforehand with an accountant who has had clients accused of money laundering and embezzlement.

The billionaire, Aras Agalarov, created the US company anonymously while preparing to move almost $20m into the country during the time of the presidential election campaign, according to interviews and corporate filings.

The company was set up for him in May 2016 by his Russian-born accountant, who has also managed the US finances of compatriots accused of mishandling millions of dollars. One of those clients has its own connection to the Trump Tower meeting.

In June 2016, Agalarov allegedly offered Trump's team damaging information from the Kremlin about Hillary Clinton, their Democratic opponent. The offer led Trump's eldest son to hold a meeting at their Manhattan offices that is now a focus of the inquiry into Moscow's election interference by Robert Mueller, the Special Counsel.

Agalarov's previously unreported shell company is another example of intriguing financial activity around the time of the Trump Tower meeting. Mueller is looking into such activity and whether any of the money involved could have been used to fund Russian meddling in the US election, which Agalarov denies.

"It was a bad idea": music publicist was unlikely fixer of Trump Tower meeting

Scott Balber, Agalarov's attorney, said the company was formed for "real estate transactions" and did not elaborate. Ilya Bykov, the accountant, said it was created to "handle certain investment projects which never materialised."

Balber said in an email: "For the avoidance of any doubt, no Mr. Agalarov has not used his accountant—or anyone else—to commit any wrongdoing and no Mr. Agalarov has not used the money you referenced—or any other money—to fund any activity relating to the US election."

Agalarov, 62, is a Moscow-based property developer who has won major contracts from Vladimir Putin's government. He hosted Trump's 2013 Miss Universe contest at his concert hall in Moscow. A leaked opposition research dossier alleged that Russian officials obtained compromising information about the future president during his stay in the city. Trump has denied wrongdoing and claims the dossier is false.

Early in June 2016, a publicist for Agalarov and his son, Emin, said in an email to Donald Trump Jr that Agalarov had been offered "documents and information that would incriminate Hillary" by a Russian prosecutor. The publicist said the material was "part of Russia and its government's support for Mr. Trump—helped along by Aras and Emin."

On 9 June, one of Agalarov's top executives and several other Russians met Donald Trump Jr. and two other senior Trump aides at Trump Tower to discuss the offer.

A month earlier, Bykov, Agalarov's US-based accountant, had incorporated a corporation for him in Delaware, a state favored by businesses for its low taxes and protection of corporate secrecy. Agalarov was not named in the paperwork, but Bykov was listed as the company's president and director.

BuzzFeed News reported last month that Agalarov moved $19.5m from an offshore investment vehicle to a US bank account eleven days after the meeting. The transfer was reportedly flagged to US Treasury officials as suspicious. The Delaware company used the same name, Silver Valley Consulting, as the offshore vehicle.

On the day of the money transfer, Trump fired his campaign manager, Corey Lewandowski, leaving his campaign chairman, Paul Manafort, in charge. Manafort, who has extensive business links to the former Soviet Union, is now cooperating with Mueller after having been convicted of financial crimes.

Having initially said that Agalarov's Delaware company was formed to handle investments that did not materialise, Bykov later said it was actually set up specifically to receive the $19.5m money transfer, but that the money was ultimately sent to Agalarov's personal US bank account instead.

Bykov said Agalarov used some of the transferred funds to buy an apartment in Florida and to pay down personal debt. Property records from Miami-Dade county state that Agalarov bought an apartment there in April 2016, before the company was created and the money was transferred. Bykov said the money was used to buy a different apartment, but did not give details.

A sixty-year-old US citizen and graduate of New York University, Bykov leads a Manhattan-based firm that provides US legal and financial services for some of Russia's wealthiest people. Among them is Igor Krutoy, a composer and prominent Putin supporter, who was part of a consortium that tried in 2011 to develop a hotel in Latvia with Trump. Krutoy was not accused of any wrongdoing.

Bykov dismissed suggestions that Agalarov was part of Russia's election interference as "sensationalism" from critics of Trump. "Aras is a fantastic guy," he said. "A great guy. Very accomplished, very fair, very likable, very open, very down to earth, very smart."

The Trumps of Russia? How billionaire Agalarov family ended up in the spotlight

Another of Bykov's clients is separately linked to the Trump Tower meeting. Natalia Veselnitskaya, a Kremlin-linked Russian attorney who attended the meeting, was at that time representing Prevezon Holdings, a Russian investment company. Prevezon was being sued by the US government for allegedly laundering part of $230m stolen by a Russian criminal network into upscale New York condominiums.

Corporate filings to New York state regulators show that several of the Prevezon companies allegedly used for money laundering were registered to Bykov's offices.

During an interview earlier this year, Bykov first suggested that the Prevezon he worked with was a different company using a similar name, which was "selling some electronics." But he later confirmed his firm "provided bookkeeping and tax services for a short period of time" for the Prevezon pursued by the US government. The company was officially owned by Denis Katsyv, a Russian businessman.

Bykov said his firm ran checks on Katsyv, and these "did not reveal any information, negative or otherwise." He said he eventually ended the business relationship over disagreements about information that Prevezon was required to disclose for tax purposes. Bykov denied any involvement in Prevezon's alleged wrongdoing.

The justice department announced in May last year that Prevezon would pay a $5.9m settlement to halt the government's legal action. No wrongdoing was admitted and Prevezon maintained its innocence.

Bykov also managed the US financial affairs of Larisa Markus, the ex-president of Russia's Vneshprombank. Markus is now serving a nine-year prison sentence in Russia, having been convicted of embezzling about $2bn of the bank's money before it collapsed in 2016.

Vneshprombank was sued in New York by a creditor that alleged Markus used the stolen funds to pay for apartments she bought in New York through a network of shell companies. These companies were registered to Bykov's office. Separately, Bykov was subpoenaed for his records on Markus by the bank in US bankruptcy court.

The creditor's lawsuit against the bank was dismissed after a judge ruled the bank was protected by the contract between them. The bankruptcy case remains open.

Bykov said lawyers who reviewed Markus's financing for him were satisfied it was legitimate. "I have to be very, very careful, because on one hand I have a response for the client and on the other hand I have a response for the law," said Bykov. "And they're not always identical."

He said Markus was innocent and was made a scapegoat for Vneshprombank's collapse. "Larisa was a victim of what's going on in Russia," said Bykov. "Not for one second do I believe she was involved in stealing this money."

Bykov said he had no involvement in misconduct and that the vast majority of his clients had spotless records. He said: "If, out of 500 clients over 15 years, three were accused of doing something wrong, that's a pretty good number, don't you think?"

Second Trump Tower Meeting

Who's Who:
- **Erik Prince:** Informal Trump campaign adviser with long-standing Republican connections. Sister Betsy DeVos became Mr. Trump's Secretary of Education.
- **George Nader:** Lebanese-American businessman and lobbyist with strong relationships with Middle East leaders.

- **Joel Zamel:** Australian-Israeli social media expert and political scientist.

Nearly ten months after the June 2016 Trump Tower meeting with the Russian lawyer was exposed by *The New York Times*, a previously unreported but equally captivating and secretive 2016 Trump Tower meeting was unearthed. This August 2016 meeting was once again attended by Mr. Trump's son and namesake, Donald Trump Jr. Also present were the informal Trump adviser and former head of the private mercenary force Blackwater, Erik Prince, as well as George Nader, a Lebanese-American businessman and lobbyist, and an Israeli social media guru named Joel Zamel.

Mr. Prince and Mr. Nader would later reappear in the Trump-Russia story for a covert rendezvous on a small island in the Seychelles in January 2017. It was during this trip that Mr. Prince met with Kirill Dmitriev, head of the state-run Russian Direct Investment Fund. Mr. Prince has testified to congress that the meeting was a chance encounter, but subsequent news reports have claimed that the meeting was an attempt by the Trump transition to set up a backchannel to the Russian government.

Mr. Prince in his House Intelligence Committee testimony said that the meeting with Mr. Dmitriev in the Seychelles was a spontaneous twenty-minute drink at the bar at the suggestion of United Arab Emirates officials who were also on the island. Numerous reports refuted Mr. Prince's claims and stated that Mr. Mueller had collected evidence that the meeting was in fact planned in advance in an effort to establish a secret line of communication with Russian leadership. Democrats in the House of Representatives demanded that Mr. Prince return to Congress to answer for his apparent perjury.

Five months prior, in the heat of the election campaign, Mr. Prince and Mr. Nader clandestinely huddled with Donald Trump Jr. to hear a pitch from Joel Zamel, who told the Trump officials that his company could help propel Mr. Trump to the presidency.

The August 2016 Trump Tower meeting was reportedly an offer of help to the Trump campaign from the Princes of Saudi Arabia and the

UAE, relayed by Mr. Nader, who has acted as an advisor to the UAE Prince. Mr. Zamel and his secretive intelligence-gathering and social media-influencing company, Psy Group, had already drawn up a multimillion-dollar plan to manipulate social media to help Mr. Trump win the election.

52 U.S. Code § 30121 expressly prohibits "a foreign national, directly or indirectly, to make—a contribution or donation of money or other thing of value, or to make an express or implied promise to make a contribution or donation, in connection with a Federal, State, or local election." The statute also makes it illegal for anyone to solicit, accept, or receive any contribution or donation from a foreign national. Mr. Zamel, who does not have American citizenship, falls under the category of foreign national. Both sides maintain that nothing was concretely offered to the Trump campaign.

Psy Group's previous clients included Russian billionaires Oleg Deripaska and Dmitry Rybolovlev. At the time of the meeting, Paul Manafort was Mr. Trump's campaign chairman. He took the job for free, despite the fact that he owed millions of dollars to Mr. Deripaska for a previous business venture. Mr. Rybolovlev was also connected to Mr. Trump through his purchase of a Trump property in 2008 for $50 million above what Trump had spent on the mansion just forty-two months prior.

The convergence of three foreign nations or individuals offering help to the Trump campaign came at a time when WikiLeaks was ramping up its disclosures of Hillary Clinton-related emails that were stolen by the Russian government. Mr. Mueller and his team of investigators have zeroed in on whether the Russian effort was coordinated in conjunction with the plans that were developed by Psy Group, whose motto is "Shape Reality."

The meeting with Mr. Nader, representing the nations of Saudi Arabia and the UAE, and the Australian-Israeli social media expert and political scientist Joel Zamel represented yet another offer to Donald Trump Jr. to enter into a criminal conspiracy to influence the election. Whereas the Russian lawyer and her associates didn't ever get around to offering anything to the Trump campaign, Mr. Zamel and Psy Group did indeed draw up very detailed plans to help Mr. Trump win the presidency.

Psy Group created three plans for the Trump campaign:

1. Analyze the political inclinations of nearly 5,000 Republican delegates, compiling a "dossier" of each persuadable delegate and what Mr. Trump's team would have to do to win over the delegate. Psy Group would then create hundreds of fake social media accounts to deliver tailored messages to these targets to garner support for Mr. Trump (given the codename "Lion") and to weaken Mr. Cruz (codename "Bear"). "All engagement, outreach and other contact with targets will be done by Psy using authentic 3rd party voices, dedicated platforms and tailored approaches," the memo explained, "This will enable each approach to look authentic and not part of the paid campaign."
   - Price tag: $3.21M
2. After Mr. Trump successfully cleared the Republican convention, the next target was clear: Mrs. Clinton, AKA "Forest." Psy Group planned to collect information about Mrs. Clinton and her ten closest associates (to be determined by the Trump team) via open-source intelligence as well as "complementary intelligence activities." In a separate memo outlining its capabilities, Psy Group stated that it utilized cyber operations as well as human sources to collect intelligence. "At the end of the process, Lion's team will have an in-depth, comprehensive intelligence dossier on each of the intelligence targets."
   - Price tag: $400,000
3. Finally, "Project Rome." Psy Group suggested a maintained effort of controlling fake social media profiles to swing minorities, suburban women, and undecided voters from Mrs. Clinton to Mr. Trump. Among their proposed elements of the plan was a strategy to create immediate "buzz" online when positive news about Mr. Trump broke and divert attention from Mrs. Clinton's criticisms. Fake social media accounts and pages on Facebook, Twitter, and Reddit would promote Mr. Trump's candidacy. "Psy seeks to commence immediately," the document reads.
   - Price tag: Unknown

Marc Mukasey, a lawyer for Mr. Zamel and protege of Mr. Trump's lawyer Rudolph Giuliani, denied that any specific plan was directly offered to the Trump campaign or that any deal was struck.

In June 2018, Special Counsel Robert Mueller indicted fourteen Russian nationals for, among other things, having "through fraud and deceit, created hundreds of social media accounts and used them to develop certain fictitious U.S. personas into 'leader[s] of public opinion' in the United States." The indictment reads remarkably similar to the proposed Psy Group plan "Project Rome." Whether Psy Group or anyone on the Trump campaign coordinated in any way with the Russian effort remains under investigation by Mr. Mueller.

After the election, Mr. Nader paid another Mr. Zamel company, called WhiteKnight and based in the Philippines, $2 million. There are conflicting reports as to why this transaction was made, with some sources claiming that it was for an analysis of how social media campaigns helped Trump, while other sources said the payment was entirely unrelated to the campaign. Mr. Nader and Mr. Zamel appear to have given investigators different answers as to whether or not Psy Group went through with the plan to help the Trump campaign. Both men have been questioned extensively by Mr. Mueller's investigators, and Psy Group's computers in Israel have been seized.

To date, this financial transaction between Mr. Nader and Mr. Zamel months after the meeting at Trump Tower is the only known case of money changing hands where election help was offered by a foreign entity. It is, undoubtedly, the most direct evidence the public has seen of a conspiracy to break federal election laws with the help of a foreign power.

Mr. Mueller began investigating soon after Mr. Nader began to cooperate with the probe. Weeks after Mr. Nader was stopped by Mr. Mueller's investigators at Dulles Airport in Washington, the Special Counsel interviewed Psy Group employees in Israel and subpoenaed the group's banking records in Cyprus. Mr. Nader, who has appeared in multiple events that are of interest Mr. Mueller, was granted partial immunity for his cooperation with investigators.

Over a year after the meeting took place, Mr. Trump Jr. failed to

ultimately owns the private intelligence group, Protexer Limited, has links to Russian commerce.

The New York Times recently reported that Donald Trump Jr., Erik Prince, and George Nader met with the leader of Psy Group, Joel Zamel, in August 2016, in what was described as a meeting to offer help to the Trump campaign.

"The emissary, George Nader, told Donald Trump Jr. that the princes who led Saudi Arabia and the United Arab Emirates were eager to help his father win election as president," the *Times* reported. "The social media specialist, Joel Zamel, extolled his company's ability to give an edge to a political campaign."

It remains unclear whether the meeting resulted in any action. After the election, Nader allegedly paid Zamel a sum of up to $2 million for unknown reasons. Attorneys for Trump Jr. and Nader did not respond to a request for comment, and Erik Prince could not immediately be reached.

Marc Mukasey, an attorney for Zamel, issued the following statement:

"Not only are you treading over ground that has been well traversed by others to no avail, but your facts are also wrong. You're chasing ghosts and you're mischaracterizing and/or misunderstanding the probe and the terms of art associated with grand jury investigations."

When asked if he had any substantive responses to the questions posed, Mukasey did not respond.

Mukasey has previously said that Zamel "offered nothing to the Trump campaign, received nothing from the Trump campaign, delivered nothing to the Trump campaign and was not solicited by, or asked to do anything for, the Trump campaign." It is uncertain why, according to Mukasey, Zamel met with then-candidate Trump's son during the heat of the election campaign.

The meeting has drawn the intense scrutiny of Special Counsel Robert Mueller in recent months, according to one source familiar with this aspect of the investigation. In February, Mueller subpoenaed the Cypriot bank accounts of Psy Group. The same source said that the Israeli bank accounts of Psy Group have also been queried, though it is unclear if a subpoena was issued.

Documents seen by this reporter indicate that Psy Group, which operates

Influence+

PSY's proprietary influence campaigns combine unique, actionable intelligence obtained through a variety of sources with a broad range of expertise in the areas of advertising and media, public relations, guerilla marketing, SEO/SEM, ORM and more. **PSY uses this gathered intelligence and broad expertise to build highly effective, targeted, online and offline campaigns.** PSY's capabilities enable targeted audiences to be impacted and influenced by credible, trusted third parties and online avatars and platforms that maintain client discretion and operate within the law.

Influence Campaigns: Through online and offline platforms, PSY has proven experience in influencing target audiences using proprietary messaging techniques and leveraging third parties "influencers" to amplify key messages and help sway opinions. Through these campaigns, PSY helps its clients to shape a new reality in line with their strategic needs and directives.

ORM: We live in an online world. PSY excels in online reputation management (ORM). Through a structured multi-phase process, PSY can modify and improve the online appearance and search results of its clients and reconstruct the manner in which they are perceived via the Internet.

*Archived Text from Psy Group's Website Touts Its Ability
to Shape A New Reality*

under the name of "Invop Limited" in Israel, used Bank Leumi in Tel Aviv for at least a portion of its banking activities. A spokesman for the bank denied that Bank Leumi has any connection to Mueller's investigation. "Bank Leumi is not connected in any way to the mentioned investigation."

Mueller, according to various news reports and a source familiar with recent interviews, has been recently asking about Russia's role in the August 2016 meeting and whether the offer from the Middle Eastern countries coordinated with the Kremlin in offering help to the Trump campaign.

The *Times* reported that "Companies connected to Mr. Zamel also have ties to Russia. One of his firms had previously worked for oligarchs linked to

Mr. Putin, including Oleg V. Deripaska and Dmitry Rybolovlev, who hired the firm for online campaigns against their business rivals."

Exclusively obtained financial, business, and credit documents show that Psy Group has set up an extensive shell company structure with its ultimate beneficiaries hidden. As previously mentioned, Psy Group is an alias for Invop Limited, incorporated in Israel. Invop is owned fully by a Cyprus company, IOCO Limited, which is in turn owned by the British Virgin Islands company, Protexer Limited. The dizzying web of shell companies, affiliates, and managers has one constant: connections to Russia.

The aforementioned IOCO Limited in Cyprus and Protexer Limited in the British Virgin Islands both have their own connections to Russian commerce. IOCO Limited is managed in Cyprus by a holding company, which is in turn administered by two Cypriot Directors who act as affiliates for two state-owned Russian banks, and one large private bank. The two Directors, Ria Christofides and Giannakis Ermogenous, are both listed as official affiliates of Vozrozhdenie Bank, Promsvyazbank, and Avtovazbank.

As Directors of Psy Group's parent company via the holding company, Christofides and Ermogenous "have the power to decide over the activities and conduct of the company. They are involved in all of the decisions concerning the company and have to fulfill certain duties towards the enterprise and its other members." Their exact duties and/or powers for the Russian banks remains unclear.

Additionally, a subsidiary of the British Virgin Islands company that ultimately owns Psy Group is a Cyprus financial services company whose vast majority of business comes from Russia. Two of its six Directors are located in Russia, and according to an April 2018 brochure, "The Company's activities are concentrated in Cyprus (operations) and Russia (business activities)." The sample incorporation documents that that financial service company uses for new clients specifically state, "The language of communications shall be English or Russian upon the choice of the Client, all the documents shall be executed in English or in English and Russian."

Notably, there is no record of any of the entities connected to Psy Group's ownership structure having any ties to Israel. Hundreds of pages of documents have been reviewed and, apart from Invop Limited in Tel Aviv, there has been zero mention of Israel.

The ultimate owner of Psy Group is unknown. The trail runs cold in the

British Virgin Islands, where the Financial Services Commission confirmed that the financial records on shareholders were filed confidentially, obstructing them from public view.

The full picture of Psy Group's complicated ownership raises new questions about who finances the group and who was behind the August 2016 Trump Tower meeting.

Peter Carr, a spokesman for the Special Counsel's office, declined to comment on their ongoing investigation.

————

Determined, yet skeptical that I could find who owned Protexer Limited, and thus who owned Psy Group, I reached out via email to the British Virgin Islands Financial Services Commission. They confirmed to me that the owners of Protexer requested anonymity, so the government was legally prohibited from sharing any details about the persons involved with the company.

My options for trying to crack the case of Protexer Limited (and thus the ultimate owner of Psy Group) were limited. Through a company database search engine, I was able to determine that Protexer Limited was the owner of at least six companies, including Psy Group. Each of these companies was unique and had no apparent connection to one another, apart from the fact that they were all based in Cyprus.

Through the meticulous process of digging through hundreds of pages of (admittedly somewhat dull!) business filings, I made the discovery I was searching for: one of the six companies owned by Psy Group's parent group was controlled by a Russian billionaire, Mikhail Slipenchuk. It is extremely rare, if not unheard of, for a subsidiary of a parent group to be controlled by a person who doesn't also own the larger conglomerate.

In plain English: the likelihood that Mr. Slipenchuk or one of his fellow Russian billionaires ultimately has some sort of financial interest in Psy Group is high.

————

June 25th, 2018:
Psy Group Sister Company Controlled by Russian Billionaire

An analysis of one of the other subsidiary companies of Protexer, MGTM Financial Services Limited, has revealed that it is controlled by the Metropol Group in Moscow, a multi-billion dollar Russian consortium. A preliminary investigation into Protexer's four other subsidiaries is still underway.

A 2016 Disclosure and Market Discipline Report prepared by MGTM confirms that "[t]he company is under the common control of Metropol Group that operates in such sectors as stock brokering, asset management, consulting, commercial banking, non-financial investing, mining, setting up industrial holdings, real estate and running a network of tour agencies."

Additionally, the MGTM website was registered by a Metropol employee, and the two original Directors of MGTM were Metropol's COO and head of debt instruments.

Domain	
Domain	mgtmfs.com
Words in	mgtmfs
Title	M.G.T.M. Financial Services Limited
Date creation	2015-06-19
Web age	3 years and 7 months
IP Address	188.40.30.49
IP Geolocation	DE Germany

Registrant		from last whois record
Name	Olga Kuznetsova	
Organization	Mgtmfs	
Email	gerder2010(at)gmail.com	
Address	Vasili Vryionides Str. 6, 2nd floor, 3095, Limas	
City	Limassol	
Country	CY Cyprus	
Phone	+35725365023	
Private	no	

Metropol is controlled by Russian billionaire Mikhail Slipenchuk, a member of the State Duma in Vladimir Putin's United Russia party from 2011—early 2016. After Slipenchuk's offshore empire was revealed in 2016 by the

Panama Papers, the businessman decided to not seek re-election to the Duma. Though not considered one of Russia's top oligarchs connected to Putin, Slipenchuk is well-connected in Russia's business and political worlds.

Slipenchuk's control of MGTM raises new questions about Metropol's relationship with Psy Group's parent company Protexer. Two financial experts with decades of experience with whom I spoke couldn't remember an instance of a subsidiary company being controlled by someone without the parent company being controlled by the same person. At the time of this publication, however, there are no direct links between the parent company of Psy Group, Protexer, and the Metropol Group.

Trident Trust in Cyprus is the ultimate owner of Psy Group

The trail of shell companies in the ownership structure of Psy Group ultimately ends with the Cyprus branch of Trident Trust. Protexer is listed alongside fifteen other subsidiaries of Trident in Cyprus, a provider of corporate, trust and fund administration services to the financial services sector. Trident services thousands of companies worldwide, but its branch in Cyprus acts as the sole shareholder for just sixteen companies in Cyprus and the British Virgin Islands.

An investigation into all of the sixteen aforementioned companies has unearthed connections to Russian banking and/or commerce in every company with the exception of Psy Group's parent company, Protexer, where public information is scant.

- Five of the sixteen companies are affiliates or Directors of Slipenchuk-connected banks/companies.
- Three of the sixteen companies have Directors that are affiliates of multiple large Russian banks.
- One of the sixteen companies used the same secretarial service (Inter Jura) as Paul Manafort in Cyprus.

Multiple requests for comment from Trident Trust over a period of weeks were not answered.

Previous owners of Psy Group

The immediate owner of Psy Group, as previously reported, is IOCO

Limited in Cyprus. Before being owned by Protexer (since 7/2016), IOCO was owned by Prime Nominees Limited (8/15–7/16) and Sea Holdings Limited (10/14–8/15), both registered in the British Virgin Islands.

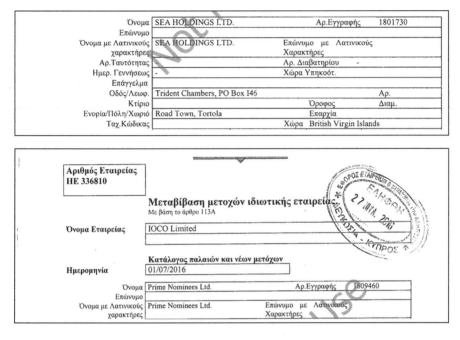

Hundreds of pages of documents reviewed from government databases show that Prime Nominees and Sea Holdings were both under the control of a Swiss lawyer and financial expert, Judith Hamburger.

Hamburger currently works for thirty companies in Panama and previously worked for two companies in the UK that remain active. Panamanian companies are not required to disclose their shareholders, making it impossible to discover for whom Hamburger ultimately works.

In the UK, however, businesses are now required to inform the government and public of their beneficial ownership. For the two active companies in which Hamburger acted as a Director and Secretary from 2010–2016, Basel Properties Limited and Lucksoft Management Limited, the beneficial owner is a Russian national by the name of Alina Zolotova. Zolotova is the wife of fugitive Russian banker Georgy Bedzhamov. Bedzhamov fled Russia for Monaco in December 2015 after allegedly embezzling $3.4 billion from his bank, Vneshprombank. Moscow courts have issued an arrest warrant for Bedzhamov, and are actively seeking his extradition.

Hamburger acting on behalf of Sea Holdings and the parent company of Prime Nominees, Cornell Enterprises

A 2012 filing showed that Bedzhamov was the ultimate beneficial owner of Basel Properties.

BASEL PROPERTIES LIMITED

NOTES TO THE ABBREVIATED ACCOUNTS

YEAR ENDED 30 NOVEMBER 2011

1. **FIXED ASSETS**

	Tangible Assets $
COST	
At 1 December 2010	12,585,715
Additions	1,976,021
At 30 November 2011	14,561,736
DEPRECIATION	–
NET BOOK VALUE	
At 30 November 2011	14,561,736
At 30 November 2010	12,585,715

2. **CONTROLLING PARTY**

The company was under the control of Mr G Bedzhamov throughout the current year and the previous year by virtue of him controlling the whole of the issued share capital

Hamburger did not respond to a request for comment. It is unclear of whom she was acting on behalf when she had control of IOCO. Furthermore, it is uncertain, though possible, that she has control of Protexer, Psy Group's parent company. Protexer uses the same P.O. Box as Sea Holdings, the original owner of IOCO (and therefore Psy Group). She has not been accused of any wrongdoing.

Hamburger's business partner

For years, Hamburger worked for Sinitus AG, a financial services company based in Switzerland under her boss Urs Meisterhans. A 2004 court document showed that Hamburger acted as legal counsel and compliance officer for Sinitus under the founder and principal, Meisterhans.

> 49.   On May 15, 2002 Mrs Judith Hamburger wrote (in her capacity of in-house legal counsel and compliance officer) on behalf of Sinitus to SCG Jersey, which managed Daraydan. The letter stated

In dozens of companies in Panama, Cyprus, and the United Kingdom, Meisterhans has worked alongside Hamburger, the woman who previously controlled Psy Group's parent company. In fact, it is uncommon to find a company in which Hamburger worked *without* Meisterhans.

In May 2015, the Swiss Prosecutor's Office indicted Meisterhans on multiple charges, including "aggravated money laundering," for his role in a massive market manipulation scheme. The principals of the money laundering scheme "would not have been able to launder the Penny Stock Scheme proceeds without the help of Urs Meisterhans," according to the court report. There is no indication at the time of this publication that Meisterhans has any direct connection to Psy Group, apart from his close association with Hamburger.

The August 2016 meeting in Trump Tower involving Donald Trump Jr., Erik Prince, George Nader, and Joel Zamel of Psy Group has drawn the intense scrutiny of Special Counsel Robert Mueller. Mueller has subpoenaed bank records in Cyprus in his aggressive pursuit of understanding the money flows behind the secretive group.

Zamel, whose companies have previously worked for Russian oligarchs such as Oleg Deripaska and Dmitry Rybolovlev, is cooperating with investigators, according to multiple media reports.

Subsequent Information

The tale of the Trump Tower meetings, as well as the story of Psy Group's involvement with the Trump campaign, has continued to evolve and remains a key part of Mr. Mueller's investigation.

In October 2018, it was revealed that Rick Gates, Mr. Manafort's associate and the eventual Deputy Campaign Chairman for the Trump campaign, solicited proposals from Psy Group. In response to this solicitation, Psy Group drew up the three aforementioned plans to help Mr. Trump defeat Mr. Cruz and later-on Mrs. Clinton.

The new reporting shifted the timeline of Psy Group's first contact with the Trump campaign from the August meeting at Trump Tower all the way back to March of 2016, when Mr. Gates first learned of the company. Mr. Gates is cooperating with Mr. Mueller's investigation and has provided crucial evidence that could implicate other members of the Trump campaign.

"Mr. Nader and Mr. Zamel have given differing accounts over whether Mr. Zamel ultimately carried out the social media effort to help the Trump campaign and why Mr. Nader paid him $2 million after the election," *The New York Times* reported in the October story about Mr. Gates's involvement with Psy Group.

"The reason for the payment has been of keen interest to Mr. Mueller, according to people familiar with the matter."

Ms. Veselnitskaya was indicted in January 2019 for Obstruction of Justice in the previously mentioned Russian money laundering case out of the Southern District of New York. Although unrelated to the June 2016 Trump Tower meeting, the nineteen-page indictment revealed some clues that may be an ominous warning for the senior members of the Trump campaign who took the meeting with the Russian lawyer.

The indictment highlighted Ms. Veselnitskaya's relationship with the office of Yuri Chaika—the Prosecutor General of Russia. New York prosecutors alleged that Mrs. Veselnitskaya carefully coordinated with, and received direction from, Mr. Chaika's office in responding to the money laundering charges. Ms. Veselnitskaya and the Prosecutor General's office then took steps to hide their close coordination. Mr. Chaika is one of the most powerful figures in Mr. Putin's government.

"The VESELNITSKAYA Declaration did not disclose that . . . VESELNITSKAYA, the defendant, in fact had access to drafts of the Russian response provided by a representative of the Prosecutor General's Office . . ." New York prosecutors wrote, "or that VESELNITSKAYA received assistance from the Prosecutor General's Office concerning the filing of a legal complaint . . ."

Abstract

The 2016 Trump Tower meetings with a Russian government-connected lawyer and later an Israeli internet expert represent two efforts by the Trump campaign to break federal law.

The meeting with Ms. Veselnitskaya and her three Russian associates was predicated upon a promise of opposition research/political dirt on Mr. Trump's opponent, Mrs. Clinton. Under federal election law, it is illegal to accept anything of value from a foreign national during a campaign. Mr. Trump Jr.'s eagerness to accept such opposition research (for which campaigns pay millions of dollars in the United States) from a foreign national signified his willingness to break the law.

Although by all public accounts, the dirt on Mrs. Clinton was never handed over to the Trump campaign, the meeting demonstrated attempted collusion. What's more, the mere fact that the Russian government managed to have three of the most senior members of Mr. Trump's team agree to such a meeting provided them with compromising material that they could potentially use to influence the decision-making of Mr. Trump's campaign and later his presidency.

When Mr. Trump Jr., just two months after hearing from Ms. Veselnitskaya, attended a meeting in Trump Tower with Joel Zamel and George Nader, it became clear that the leaders of the Trump campaign were willing to do whatever it took to beat Mrs. Clinton. The first get-together with foreign nationals in Trump Tower could possibly be explained by ignorance, but the second meeting proved Mr. Trump Jr.'s disregard for the law.

My research into these two meetings established the fact that Mr. Trump himself knew at least five of the eight people who attended the June meeting, making it increasingly unlikely that he didn't know such a meeting was taking place. Furthermore, my deep-diving into the corporate documents of Mr. Zamel's Psy Group called into question the true ownership of the firm and indicated that Russian money may have secretly funded the social media-manipulation company.

The Coffee Boy and His Mysterious Wife

Who's Who:

- **George Papadopoulos:** Former Trump campaign foreign policy adviser.
- **Joseph Mifsud:** Maltese professor who is well-connected to Russian government officials.
- **Sergei Millian:** Belarusian-American businessman who previously worked alongside Mr. Trump.
- **Simona Mangiante Papadopoulos:** Wife of Mr. Papadopoulos, who also worked for Mr. Mifsud in 2016, before meeting her soon-to-be husband.

Overview

The first person charged with a crime relating to the Russian interference in the 2016 election was a little-known young foreign policy adviser to Mr. Trump named George Papadopoulos.

Mr. Papadopoulos, who turned twenty-nine-years-old during the campaign, was charged by federal authorities in July 2017 for lying to the FBI about his contacts with an alleged professor-turned-Russian agent of Maltese descent. Mr. Papadopoulos quickly pleaded guilty and agreed to cooperate with Mr. Mueller's probe.

When it began to appear that Mr. Trump was indeed going to be the Republican nominee in March 2016, the candidate hastily began assembling a foreign policy team. In a late-March interview with the

Washington Post, Mr. Trump named Mr. Papadopoulos as part of his team, saying, "George is an oil and gas consultant; excellent guy."

Before being thrust onto the national and international stage by having the presumptive Republican nominee name him to the *Post*, Mr. Papadopoulos was not well-known in political circles. Following his graduation from DePaul University, he went abroad and completed a Master of Science degree in security studies from University College London. His first job was as an unpaid intern at the Conservative Washington, DC think tank the Hudson Institute. For four years, Mr. Papadopoulos stayed at the Hudson Institute in an unpaid role, publishing opinion-editorial pieces in various newspapers around the world. Near the end of 2015, Mr. Papadopoulos landed a position at a London energy consultancy.

His political career began when the Ben Carson campaign hired him as a National Security and Foreign Policy Advisor. He would leave the campaign after just four months, after Carson's chances at securing the nomination quickly faded. Mr. Papadopoulos was then hired by the London Centre of International Law Practice (LCILP), where the aforementioned Maltese professor held a senior position.

While still employed by LCILP, Mr. Papadopoulos was interviewed by Trump national co-chairman Sam Clovis. During this interview, according to Mr. Mueller's prosecutors, Mr. Clovis made it clear that a main objective of the Trump campaign was to improve relations with Russia. Shortly after this job interview, Mr. Papadopoulos was mentioned by Mr. Trump in the *Washington Post* article.

Mr. Papadopoulos kept his position at LCILP and took a work trip to a university in Rome, where he met the Maltese professor, Joseph Mifsud. Only after learning that Mr. Papadopoulos was also working as an advisor to Mr. Trump did Mr. Mifsud take any interest in the young energy consultant. Mr. Papadopoulos, eager to make a name for himself in the political world, found an opportunity to advance the objective of improving Russian relations as described to him by Mr. Clovis when he learned that Mr. Mifsud had high-level contacts within the Russian government.

Mr. Mifsud took a keen interest in Mr. Papadopoulos, and they met multiple times throughout March and April 2016. In one March meeting, Mr. Papadopoulos was under the impression that Mr. Mifsud brought along President Vladimir Putin's niece (the woman turned out to be just a Russian student). Nevertheless, Mr. Papadopoulos was told that she was Mr. Putin's niece, and that did not stop the Trump adviser from attending the meeting.

During an April breakfast with Mr. Papadopoulos, Mr. Mifsud shared information from his recent trip to Moscow that would spark the entire Russia investigation. It was at this breakfast, on a very cold Tuesday morning in London, that Mr. Mifsud dropped a bomb that altered the course of history forever: the Russian government had dirt on Hillary Clinton in the form of thousands of emails.

What happened next is still under dispute. Mr. Papadopoulos, to this day, claims that he cannot remember telling anyone on the Trump campaign about the monumental news that Mr. Mifsud shared with him. He did, however, according to his own account, tell the Greek Foreign Minister, and according to Mr. Mueller's prosecutors, an Australian diplomat named Alexander Downer.

After WikiLeaks began leaking emails sent by Mrs. Clinton in July, Mr. Downer contacted the FBI to tell them what he had heard from Mr. Papadopoulos just weeks prior. The FBI launched its investigation into the Russian interference and possible coordination with the Trump campaign on July 31, 2016.

Sometime in the summer of 2016, Mr. Papadopoulos received a message out of the blue from a Belarusian-American businessman and shadowy figure, Sergei Millian. Mr. Millian for years ran the Russian-American Chamber of Commerce in the USA, a small, obscure company that connected businessmen in Russia and the United States. In 2008, Mr. Millian allegedly partnered with Mr. Trump in an effort to sell units to Russian investors for the Trump Hollywood development. Mr. Millian in interviews with Russian media would brag about his close relationship with Mr. Trump up until early 2017, when both he and the Trump team sought to distance themselves from one another.

The educational and professional background of Mr. Millian, who changed his name from Siarhei Kukuts to Sergio Millian and later Sergei Millian, remains cloudy. Various resumes posted online tell two different stories: One resume showed that Mr. Millian attended college in Belarus and worked for the Belarusian government as a translator and businessman. The other resume, under the name Sergei Kukuts, said that he attended school at Moscow State Linguistic University in Russia and worked for the Russian Ministry of Foreign Affairs. These discrepancies, as well as his odd "Chamber of Commerce" company, have led at least some investigators to consider the possibility that Mr. Millian is connected to Russian intelligence.

Paul Joyal, the managing director of National Strategies, told ABC News that the Russian-American Chamber of Commerce reminded him of a "classic Soviet front organization."

"Front organization have been a platform for spotting and assessing potential intelligence recruitment and collection targets," he said. "They commonly used sponsored trips as a means of making contact and sometimes developing or compromising intelligence targets of interest."

With his bizarre background a simple Google search away, Mr. Millian, in July of 2016, reached out to Mr. Papadopoulos on LinkedIn and the two met in Manhattan. Through the rest of 2016, Mr. Millian and Mr. Papadopoulos corresponded regularly and met in person multiple times, per media reports. The exact nature of their discussions has, like many other things in Mr. Millian's life, been subject to multiple versions of events and changing narratives.

There appear to have been at least three different explanations as to why Mr. Papadopoulos and Mr. Millian had such regular contact in 2016 after not knowing one another before. The first story, as told by Mr. Papadopoulos's wife, was that Mr. Millian offered Mr. Papadopoulos a $30,000 monthly retainer on the condition he remain attached to the campaign. Then, the story was that Mr. Papadopoulos was offered a job working for the Russian oil company Bashneft, which is owned by the energy conglomerate Rosneft. This possibility is the most intriguing for multiple reasons.

A month prior to the outreach, Mr. Millian attended the St. Petersburg International Economic Forum in Russia. He was pictured with the Russian oligarch Oleg Deripaska and Alexander Novak, the Minister of Energy. His connection to Mr. Novak signals that Mr.

Millian has the relationship to have potentially offered a job working for a state-owned oil company to Mr. Papadopoulos.

Then, just weeks before Mr. Millian reached out to Mr. Papadopoulos on LinkedIn, another Trump adviser, Carter Page, made a sudden trip to Moscow. An ex-British spy, Christopher Steele, who was compiling intelligence reports that would come to be known as the Trump Dossier, would later write a memo in which he alleged that Trump campaign members were offered the brokerage fee of an upcoming sale of some of Rosneft's shares.

"[Rosneft CEO] offered PAGE/TRUMP's associates the brokerage of up to a 19 per cent (privatised) stake in Rosneft in return PAGE had expressed interest . . ." Steele wrote. The sale did go through in December (just as Page made another trip to Moscow) and the buyers of the Rosneft shares remain unknown today.

If Mr. Millian did indeed offer Mr. Papadopoulos some sort of business proposal with a Rosneft subsidiary, then Mr. Steele's report would look increasingly accurate.

Finally, in a late-2018 interview, Mr. Papadopoulos claimed that Mr. Millian's offer was not working on any energy-related deal, but rather doing "PR work for an ex Russian minister." It's important to note that Mr. Papadopoulos has no professional experience doing any public relations work. Mr. Millian's interactions with Mr. Papadopoulos remain under intense scrutiny by congressional investigators.

Through the rest of the 2016 campaign, Mr. Papadopoulos also attempted to leverage Mr. Mifsud's Russian contacts to set up a meeting between Mr. Trump and Mr. Putin. Mr. Mifsud introduced Mr. Papadopoulos to a Russian think-tank leader who had multiple connections to the Russian Ministry of Foreign Affairs. Although the meeting never took place, Mr. Papadopoulos kept his campaign supervisors abreast of his efforts. Mr. Papadopoulos did manage to arrange a meeting between Mr. Trump and the Egyptian President Abdel Fattah el-Sisi.

Two days before the election, Mr. Papadopoulos spoke to a group of Greeks in New York City, and proclaimed, "Mr. Trump and my team thought it was important for me to be here."

Sometime during the final weeks of the 2016 campaign, we would later learn, Mr. Papadopoulos was contacted via LinkedIn by a young, blonde Italian woman named Simona Mangiante, who also happened to work for Mr. Mifsud at LCILP. The two continued to trade messages back and forth before meeting in person in the Spring of 2017. They quickly got engaged and took a weeks-long honeymoon in Europe, hobnobbing with foreign business leaders.

It was during this honeymoon that an Israeli consultant paid Mr. Papadopoulos $10,000 in cash, allegedly as part of a business offer. Family members of Mr. Papadopoulos became so concerned that this consultant, Charles Tawil, was acting on behalf of a foreign intelligence agency that they took the money from Mr. Papadopoulos and locked it in a safe. Mr. Papadopoulos would later claim, without any evidence, that Mr. Tawil was acting on behalf of Western intelligence agencies in an effort to entrap him. Without the means to continue the honeymoon with his new fiancée, Mr. Papadopoulos flew back home to Chicago, where he was arrested at the airport by FBI agents.

Ms. Mangiante soon followed, and was herself questioned by Mr. Mueller's prosecutors about her work for Mr. Mifsud and their suspicions that she might be acting as a Russian spy. The Mueller team, according to Ms. Mangiante's account, believed that her previous work for the European Parliament may have just been a cover for her spying. She has vigorously denied these allegations.

With Mr. Papadopoulos cooperating with federal investigators, Ms. Mangiante acted as an unofficial spokeswoman for her fiancé. "I believe history will remember him like John Dean," Ms. Mangiante said in a January 2018 interview, referring to the former Nixon lawyer who cooperated with Watergate investigators. Mr. Papadopoulos and Ms. Mangiante married in March 2018, and then Ms. Mangiante's tune suddenly changed. By mid-2018, she was claiming that her husband was set up and entrapped by Western intelligence agencies. No longer was he the John Dean of the Russia investigation, but rather a patsy used by the FBI, CIA, and British intelligence to infiltrate and spy on the Trump campaign.

Her rapid change in opinion and tone was consistent with someone who was attempting to spread disinformation and muddy the waters.

I found myself disturbed by her actions and frustrated that journalists weren't closely examining who this woman truly was.

With the knowledge of Mr. Papadopoulos's various activities in 2016, it came as a shock when, after Mr. Papadopoulos's guilty plea was revealed to the public in October 2017, members of the Trump team began to downplay his role during the campaign. Former Trump campaign adviser Michael Caputo appeared on CNN the day the indictment was released and infamously stated, "He was the coffee boy . . . he had nothing to do with the campaign."

The blatant lie that Mr. Caputo uttered on CNN upset and surprised me. I saw it as a pivotal moment in American history. Was the media going to dig in and research the daily life of Mr. Papadopoulos during the campaign and comprehensively rebuke Mr. Caputo's falsehoods? Or were we going to take these political advisors at their word, and not do the due diligence?

To my disdain, hours turned into days and the coffee-boy narrative began to resonate. Seeing a lack of real investigative journalism into this energy advisor's background and activities during the 2016 campaign, I decided to do my own research and share it with as many people as possible who would take a college student seriously. As Ms. Mangiante began to spread conspiracy theories about her husband later on in 2018, I began investigating her background as well.

The result was a series of articles, first on Mr. Papadopoulos in November of 2017, and then on Ms. Mangiante in 2018, doing a deep-dive on the background of these two individuals in an attempt to a) refute the obvious mistruths relayed by the Trump campaign, and b) find out who Ms. Mangiante really was and why she and her new husband began to espouse conspiracy theories about our own intelligence agents.

The Process

Fairly new to investigations, I started where anyone would start: Google. Doing a reverse image search of the few public pictures of Mr. Papadopoulos proved to be a goldmine. I found pictures in Greek media of Mr. Papadopoulos having high-level meetings with leaders from Greece, Cyprus, and Israel. This was the basis of my first article.

He was no coffee boy.

November 3, 2017
Exclusive: Papadopoulos Had a Much Greater Role than the White House Admits, Including a Meeting With the Greek President
The one-on-one meeting took place in the Spring of 2016

George Papadopoulos, the former Trump adviser who was arrested in July by Special Counsel Robert Mueller for lying to the FBI, had a much more prominent and important role on the Trump team than the White House has portrayed. Evidence exists that George Papadopoulos had a direct line to Donald Trump as late as December, 2016. This implies that the White House has not only lied about the high-level role that Papadopoulos had, but that the President himself is wildly misreporting the facts when he stated that "Few people knew the young, low level volunteer named George."

Beginning in the Spring of 2016, Papadopoulos had a series of meetings with the most senior levels of the Greek political world. To this day unreported by US media, Papadopoulos had a one-on-one meeting with the President of Greece, Prokopis Pavlopoulos.

The importance of this meeting cannot be overstated. The Trump team has tried to cast Papadopoulos as a "coffee boy", someone who did little for the Trump campaign and had no real role. The President of Greece is reported to have "received Papadopoulos as a person who would potentially help Greece, if Trump was elected." The role Papadopoulos was playing for the campaign was not a coffee boy, it was as a senior foreign policy adviser to the Republican nominee. The discussion was held in the Presidential Mansion in Athens, Greece.

In November 2016, after Donald Trump was declared the winner of the election, Greek Defense Minister Panos Kammenos tweeted his congratulations, underscoring how important of a role Papadopoulos plays for Greece-US relations. Later that year, in December, Papadopoulos went back to Greece as a representative of the President-elect Donald Trump and had two highly significant meetings.

First, he met with the Greek Defense Minister. After his lunch with Kammenos, Papadopoulos spoke to local Greek news. "On December 4, speaking to local Greek TV stations in Northern Greece, Papadopoulos was reluctant to discuss details of the US policy towards Greece, Turkey and the Balkans saying that 'as a representative of the president-elect' he was not yet in position to discuss policy details." *Star* Northern Greece referred to Papadopoulos as "one of the closest aides to [the] newly elected President Trump."

This crucial interview again discredits the White House. Papadopoulos was a Trump adviser representing the country on foreign land. He seemed to indicate that he was privy to the contents of the phone call between President-elect Trump and the Greek Prime Minister Alexis Tsipras, saying that it went "very well."

Secondly, Papadopoulos met with Ieronymos II, the Archbishop of Athens and All Greece. The Archbishop asked Mr. Papadopoulos to "convey his wishes to the new President of the United States for a successful term," suggesting that Papadopoulos had a direct line of communication with Donald Trump.

On January 20, Inauguration Day, Kammenos had a meeting with former Chief of Staff Reince Priebus and Papadopoulos. It is unclear whether Priebus and Papadopoulos met with the Defense Minister as a duo or separately.

Apart from Greece, Papadopoulos has ties to Israel, Cyprus, and Russia.

During the Inauguration weekend, Papadopoulos again was referred to as "Trump adviser," and met with Yossi Dagan, a high-profile Israeli settlement activist. Dagan is well known in Israeli political circles, and has met with Prime Minister Netanyahu numerous times.

On November 13, Papadopoulos was overseas again representing the Trump agenda, this time in Cyprus. He gave a lengthy interview to local Cyprus news, saying, among other things, "The US must stop the arms embargo in Cyprus." It should be noted that former Trump Campaign Chair Paul Manafort was recently indicted on twelve counts, including money laundering through bank accounts—yes—in Cyprus.

Russia

According to Papadopoulos's FBI indictment, "Based on a conversation that took place on or about March 6, 2016, with a supervisory campaign official (the "Campaign Supervisor"), defendant PAPADOPOULOS understood that a principal foreign policy focus of the Campaign was an improved U.S. relationship with Russia."

With this in mind, Papadopoulos gave an interview to the Jerusalem Post in Israel on April 7, 2016. He stated, "Trump . . . sees Russian President Vladimir Putin as a responsible actor."

Papadopoulos learned through a professor in London in late April that the Russians had dirt on Hillary Clinton, including thousands of emails. In mid-August, a Campaign Supervisor told defendant PAPADOPOULOS that "I would encourage you" and another foreign policy advisor to the Campaign to "make the trip [to Russia], if it is feasible."

The next month, Papadopoulos gave an exclusive interview to the Russian news agency Interfax. It is unclear where this interview took place. However, Papadopoulos criticized sanctions against Russia, and hinted at lifting them. He said, "Sanctions have done little more than to turn Russia towards China. It is not in the interest of the West . . ."

He also noted that Russia can be a helpful actor in NATO, Ukraine, and elsewhere. At this point, many of the hacked DNC emails had been released. Papadopoulos and an unknown number of his supervisors in the Trump campaign knew that Russia had "thousands of emails" and they knew that Russia was responsible for the DNC hack, yet they still pushed to end sanctions and improve relations.

These previously unreported meetings and circumstances cast doubt on the portrait that the White House has tried to paint about George Papadopoulos. They raise even more questions as to why the Trump team is misreporting the truth and why they insist on covering up all connections to Vladimir Putin's Russia.

One relationship that Mr. Papadopoulos appeared to find especially valuable was with the Greek Defense Minister, Panos Kammenos. Seeing that Mr. Papadopoulos and Mr. Kammenos met numerous times throughout 2016, I began to look for any nexus between the Greek leader and Russia. What I found was the kickstarter to my investigative journalism career.

Simply connecting the dots from various news articles over the years, I was able to determine that Mr. Kammenos had a very close relationship with the Kremlin. There were even concerns that Mr. Kammenos was somehow co-opted by the Russian government during a trip to Moscow in 2015. I quickly found that Mr. Kammenos was the leader of a think tank in Greece called the Institute of Geopolitical Studies. I didn't have to search through the bowels of the internet to find this fact—it was literally on his Wikipedia page.

I then made a simple Google search of the name of the think tank in quotation marks. This is an extremely handy trick in open-source investigations. By putting the search in quotation marks, the results will only include matches for the EXACT phrasing within the quotes.

One of the first hits was from TASS—a major government owned news agency in Russia. The webpage explained that Kammenos's think tank signed a Memorandum of Understanding with a Russian government-connected think tank led by a career Russian spy. Not just any think tank, but the think tank that drew up the plans to spread fake news during the 2016 US election season, per a report by *Reuters*.

The connections between Kammenos, the Russian government, and the exact think tank that came up with the plans to interfere with our election led to article number two.

Papadopoulos Met Numerous Times with Greek Leader with Substantial Ties to the Kremlin's 2016 US Interference Campaign

Throughout 2016, Trump adviser George Papadopoulos met multiple times with Greek Defense Minister Panos Kammenos, a man with connections to Russia's Foreign Intelligence Service (SVR) and Vladimir Putin himself.

On all of these occasions, Papadopoulos represented himself as a current adviser to Donald Trump. He first met the Defense Minister in the early spring, according to the Greek newspaper *Kathimerini*. He had at least one other meeting with Kammenos in the spring/summer of 2016. In stunning detail unreported by US media, the Greek publication states that Papadapoulos was let go from the campaign and then re-hired in early November, under a directive to only speak to the media about Hillary Clinton's emails. Papadapoulos also requested a one-on-one meeting with the Prime Minister of Greece. The passage is below, as translated for me by a native Greek speaker.

Two months later, Mr. Papadopoulos comes to Athens and meets the President of Greece, Pr. Pavlopoulos. He uploaded indeed on his personal website page a picture of the meeting where it appears that he requested a direct meeting with the office of the Prime Minister. Finally he was able to see only Mr. Kammenos. He also met, on one of his trips, Mr. Kosta Karamali.

Two weeks prior to the elections we contacted again Mr. Papadopoulos, where he informed us that he "had left the campaign" because "he had done his part." One week later, he told us that he had returned again, but that he was under direction that no one could speak to the Press about any topic except for the FBI's investigation of the emails of Ms. Clinton. Although it is not clear exactly which—but also how close—is his relationship to Trump, just two days before the election, he took the airplane from Chicago to attend an event in Astoria (Greek town in NYC). "Mr. Trump thought that it was important for me to come and speak to you," he says in his introduction.

This passage brings up more questions than answers. Why was Papadapoulos originally let go and why did the Trump campaign find it so essential to spread dirt on Hillary Clinton that they brought him back a week later? Who ordered this directive? Who ordered Papadapoulos to fly to New York to speak to the Greek community about Hillary Clinton's emails as an official member of the Trump campaign two days before the election? Why was this so important to them? Papadopoulos strongly indicated that Mr. Trump himself wanted him to speak to the Greek group in Astoria, further eroding Mr. Trump's claim that "few people knew" him. It appears that Mr. Trump knew him on November 6, 2016 as an important, high-level adviser.

Defense Minister Kammenos saw Papadopoulos as a crucial partner as well, as evidenced by his tweet on November 9 congratulating Trump on his win.

In December, Papadopoulos met with Kammenos on two separate occasions. Kammenos, the only man in Greece whom Papadopoulos met with numerous times, has ties to Russia's Foreign Intelligence Service (SVR) and the Kremlin team that carried out the 2016 US Election interference campaign. He founded the Institute of Geopolitical Studies, which in 2014 signed a "memorandum of understanding" with the Russian Institute for Strategic Studies (RISS). A memorandum of understanding "expresses a convergence of will between [two] parties, indicating an intended common line of action."

RISS was under the control of the SVR until 2009, when Putin decided it would be best to have it under his control at the President's office. The RISS director until January 2017 was Leonid Reshetnikov, a man who is close to President Putin and regularly has meetings at the Kremlin.

In hacked messages from an influential Russian blogger in 2014, a prominent Greek blogger describes an encounter with Panos Kammenos:

> "Panos appeared almost one month ago full of 'enthusiasm,' asking for regular cooperation. And then he went to Moscow for personal reasons, as he told us (for a friend's wedding) and then disappeared from the face of the Earth in a quite impressive manner. I am very curious if I will ever know what reasons he will give for disappearing."

One month later, the memorandum of understanding was signed with Reshetnikov. After this agreement, the official positions of Kammenos mimicked Kremlin talking points. In Moscow in March 2015, Kammenos spoke of terminating Russian sanctions.

That wedding, the *Wall Street Journal* reported, was the result of an invitation from Russian businessman Konstantin Malofeev. Malofeev is barred from traveling to Europe or the United States because of allegations that he acted in support of the destabilization of Eastern Ukraine. Needless to say, he is strongly linked to the Kremlin. The *Foreign Times* summed it up by saying in 2015 that, "Nikos Kotzias, the foreign minister, and Panos Kammenos, defence minister, have both been cultivated by figures close to Russian president Vladimir Putin's inner circle." This was a year after Kammenos's mysterious trip to Moscow.

In April 2017, *Reuters* reported that a Putin-linked think tank drew up plans to sway the 2016 US election, citing confidential documents. That Putin-linked think tank? Leonid Reshetnikov's RISS.

This Reshetnikov-Kammenos-Papadapoulos chain is a direct line of officials connecting the Kremlin's US election interference to the Trump team.

The *Reuters* report focused on two highly confidential RISS documents that US intelligence had received:

> It recommended the Kremlin launch a propaganda campaign on social media and Russian state-backed global news outlets to encourage U.S. voters to elect a president who would take a softer line toward Russia than the administration of then-President Barack Obama, the seven officials said.
>
> A second institute document, drafted in October and distributed in the same way, warned that Democratic presidential candidate Hillary Clinton was likely to win the election. For that reason, it argued, it was better for Russia to end its pro-Trump propaganda and instead intensify its messaging about voter fraud to undermine the U.S. electoral system's legitimacy and damage Clinton's reputation in an effort to undermine her presidency, the seven officials said.

On one of his first trips to Greece, Papadopoulos also met with former Prime Minister Kostas Karamanlis. Karamanlis, in a surprising turn of events, was wiretapped by American officials because of his close ties to the Kremlin. The wiretaps also uncovered "an alleged plot to assassinate Karamanlis and found that there was evidence to suggest that persons unknown had targeted the premier because of his attempts to pursue closer relations with Russia."

Wikileaks, which the US has deemed a hostile intelligence service helped by the Kremlin, published the intelligence cables. The Wikileaks reports state that the close ties between Greece and Russia "provoked action by the United States to avert agreements for Russian pipelines, leading to the gradual abandonment of the plans by Athens and its commitment to the Trans-Adriatic Pipeline (TAP), as well as the cancellation of plans to acquire Russian military equipment."

This cancellation likely cost Vladimir Putin's Russia billions of dollars, leaving him with a deep-seated anger towards the United States. With these revelations in 2015, Putin set his sights on the upcoming US election.

———

Finally, in an attempt to once and for all squash the narrative that Mr. Papadopoulos was a coffee boy, I came up with an out-of-the-box idea: Email as many foreign governments as possible and see if Mr. Papadopoulos had any interaction with diplomats. I sent forty emails to most of the countries that comprise Europe.

I got exactly one response, but it was a substantive, newsworthy answer. The UK foreign affairs office confirmed to me, on background, that Mr. Papadopoulos had a working-level meeting with a UK official in September 2016. This proved that well after the contacts with Mr. Mifsud, Mr. Papadopoulos was doing official Trump campaign business with foreign governments. It also poured cold water on any remaining assertion that Mr. Papadopoulos didn't play an important role in Mr. Trump's team.

This meeting was my next story on the "coffee boy."

———

November 8, 2017

Exclusive: Papadopoulos Had Working-Level Meeting with U.K. Foreign Office in September 2016

The official meeting has not previously been reported.

George Papadopoulos had a working-level meeting with a U.K. Foreign and Commonwealth Office (FCO) official in September 2016, according to two U.K. government sources. Previously, the public was only aware of one Papadopoulos trip to London in November of 2016, during which he met briefly with some lower-level representatives of the FCO as part of their normal outreach to both US Presidential candidates.

According to the two UK government sources, who spoke on condition of anonymity to more freely discuss the topic, Papadopoulos had a one-on-one *working-level meeting* with the unnamed FCO official. The meeting took place with an unidentified, high-ranking member of the UK's department that handles foreign affairs.

There are three immensely important points to draw from this previously unreported meeting:

One, a working-level meeting means that Papadopoulos and the FCO official had substantive talks; it was not simply to exchange pleasantries. They likely discussed policy and Trump's positions on various aspects of foreign policy, per one of the U.K. government sources. This is the first confirmation that Papadopoulos had a major role in the Trump foreign policy team, especially with one of the United States' important and steadfast allies. Since the news of Papadopoulos's arrest became public, White House officials and people in President Trump's orbit have consistently tried to downplay his role in the campaign:

Sarah Huckabee Sanders, Press Secretary, October 30:
"It was extremely limited. It was a volunteer position. And again, no activity was ever done in an official capacity on behalf of the campaign. He was a volunteer on the campaign."

President Trump, October 31:
"Few people knew the young, low level volunteer named George."

Corey Lewandowski, former Trump Campaign Manager, October 31:

"George was a low-level volunteer who might have attended a meeting of the foreign policy advisory team. He was not a person who was involved with the day-to-day operations of the campaign, or a person who I recall interacting with."

Michael Caputo, former Trump Campaign Aide, October 31:

"He was a coffee boy. He had nothing to do with the campaign."

With these new revelations, all of these statements have been proven inaccurate. He participated in official activities on behalf of the Trump campaign. He was not a low-level volunteer; he was involved with the operations of the campaign. He was not a coffee boy, unless they simply have amazing coffee in Greece, Cyprus, Israel, and the U.K.

Two, it casts doubt on the role of other members on the Trump campaign. If the White House is willing to blatantly mischaracterize the role that Papadopoulos played during the campaign, why wouldn't they do the same with others such as Carter Page, Roger Stone, and Sam Clovis? And it brings up a larger question—what are they trying to hide? With this news, their credibility on all things Russia has been severely weakened, if not destroyed.

Lastly, London is extremely significant in the Trump/Russia story. From the Papadopoulos indictment, we know that London was the agreed-upon location for a meeting with the Russian ambassador (which never happened, according to the FBI). The indictment mentions Papadopoulos being in London in March and meeting a professor named Joseph Mifsud and an unnamed female Russian national.

In April, Papadopoulos emailed Sam Clovis, attempting to set up a Trump-Putin meeting by saying, "the advantage of being in London is that these governments tend to speak a bit more openly in 'neutral' cities." Later that month, Papadopoulos flew back to London and learned through Mifsud that the Russians had "dirt" on Hillary Clinton. The indictment has no mention of Papadopoulos being in London in September. I am unaware if the FBI or the Special Counsel's office knows of this fact.

Also in London are two more major players in the Trump/Russia narrative: Julian Assange and Nigel Farage.

Assange is the founder of Wikileaks, the organization that published the hacked D.N.C. and John Podesta emails. Nigel Farage was a British politician who in June was named a person of interest to the FBI in the Russia investigation because of his relationship with members of the Trump team and Mr. Assange. In March, Trump associate Roger Stone tweeted that he had a back channel to Assange:

> "@RVAwonk you stupid stupid bitch-never denied perfectly legal back channel to Assange who indeed had the goods on #CrookedHillary"

Was his back channel through Farage?

Simona Mangiante Papadopoulos

After a few more supplemental reports on Mr. Papadopoulos, my attention and focus was on Trump Tower Moscow, as previously discussed.

However, in 2018, when Ms. Mangiante, now Mrs. Papadopoulos, started to spread obvious disinformation, I became suspicious. In September, Mrs. Papadopoulos acknowledged that Mr. Mueller's team suspected her of being a Russian spy. This piece of news was enough for me to turn my attention back to the couple and investigate Mrs. Papadopoulos.

Her work at the same small law institution as Mr. Mifsud, LCILP, flew under the radar until the news broke about Mr. Mueller's questioning Mrs. Papadopoulos about being a Russian spy. She claimed that Mr. Mifsud never paid her for her work, so she left after just three months. Was it just a coincidence that she became a subordinate of Mr. Mifsud in the three months leading up to the 2016 election?

Many avid followers of the Trump–Russia story noted that Mrs. Papadopoulos's accent did not sound Italian, but rather Eastern European. Though intriguing and admittedly somewhat interesting, this criticism didn't hold up to my perceived standards of what deserved to be investigated. It was a subjective observation that could not be proven one way or the other. Her background, however, including her purported legal work in the United States, could be confirmed with a bit of elbow grease.

I started with her LinkedIn, the networking service where professionals of all backgrounds post their resumes. Immediately, I was struck by the fact that there were three different profiles set up for Simona Mangiante. Two were nearly blank, only listing her as a "lawyer" at "Mayer & Brown" in New York City. The other one was much more developed, listing her educational and employment history, including dates and locations.

I'd like to tell you that I developed some super-secret way of searching the internet and discovering hidden information, but that is not the case. I just spent time contacting every single employer for whom Papadopoulos said she had worked, every single school that Papadopoulos said she had attended, and every colleague with whom she had communicated. I emailed. I called. I sent messages.

It was during this process that I was contacted by a relative of Mr. Papadopoulos. For the sake of protecting his/her identity, we will call this person Alex. Alex was deeply troubled by Mrs. Papadopoulos and her shady behavior. Alex introduced me to other close relatives of Mr. Papadopoulos, who, along with Alex, were convinced that Mrs. Papadopoulos was acting on behalf of a foreign entity.

Alex made many claims about Mrs. Papadopoulos, ranging from insignificant to extraordinary. One point that Alex kept mentioning was the apparent fluidity of Mrs. Papadopoulos's age. In various interviews, Mrs. Papadopoulos gave different ages: twenty-nine, thirty-three, thirty-four. Alex told me that after a night of drinking, Mrs. Papadopoulos admitted her true birth year of 1981, which would make her thirty-seven years old.

In the middle of accumulating all of this raw intelligence, I received an email from Mayer Brown, the United States-based law firm for which Mrs. Papadopoulos claimed she worked as an Associate for fifteen months in 2007 and 2008. Specifically, the email was from Mayer Brown's lead spokesman, John Tuerck: "Our records indicate she was never employed at Mayer Brown, in any capacity."

Armed with the knowledge that she lied about the only job listed on all three of her LinkedIn profiles, I knew I was on the right track. I continued chatting with Alex as I scraped Mrs. Papadopoulos's social media accounts for any information that might be useful.

I found a tweet for a website that Mrs. Papadopoulos created in late 2016, concerning her years-long work on cases of child abductions. Though the website had since been deleted, one can often find very valuable information from the technical details of the creation of a custom domain name and page. Running what is called a "WHOIS" search on any domain name can, if the information is not protected properly, reveal facts about the user who registered the website address.

The WHOIS search for Mrs. Papadopoulos's website revealed that she listed a $1.5M flat in North London as her location as of October 2016. If Mr. Mifsud did not pay Mrs. Papadopoulos while she was in London, how could she afford to be living in such a lavish residence? The property deed showed that Mrs. Papadopoulos did not own the property, but instead likely rented at a price of approximately $4,500 per month, based on estimates.

Complicating matters was an assertion made by Alex, who said that Mrs. Papadopoulos insisted that she lived in South Kensington during her time in London. The address listed on the WHOIS search was certainly not in the South Kensington neighborhood. I took these claims to Mrs. Papadopoulos herself, who later confirmed that she had not two addresses in London, but three. With no income from LCILP, this lifestyle appeared completely perplexing.

With the backdrop of the questioning by Mr. Mueller, the lies about her employment at Mayer Brown, the discrepancies about her age, and the various concerns from friends and family were the nexus of my article on Mrs. Papadopoulos.

———

October 4, 2018
Simona Mangiante-Papadopoulos is Misleading the Public
Statements about her background don't align with the facts

The wife of former Trump adviser George Papadopoulos has garnered much attention for her media appearances, in which she proclaimed that Papadopoulos would be remembered as a John Dean figure, before completely changing her tune, claiming Papadopoulos was set up by the FBI and other allied intelligence agencies. She is the leading voice behind the conspiracy theory that the Maltese professor who told Papadopoulos about dirt on Hillary Clinton was actually working for Western intelligence. Mangiante worked for the professor from September–November 2016, according to her own accounts.

Mangiante's public persona is as intriguing and interesting as her claims about the Russia investigation. She has portrayed herself as an actress, model, fashionista, and lawyer focused on international issues, including child abduction. However, a weeks-long investigation into her international background has revealed that she isn't being truthful with at least some aspects of her background.

The revelations come as Mangiante has revealed that FBI investigators questioned her about being a Russian spy. "I used to work as a diplomat at the European Parliament for a few years and this could be a red flag because many officials at European Union actually—it's a cover-up for spy jobs," Mangiante told ABC News. She has denied that she has any affiliations with intelligence agencies or any ties to Russia.

In the years prior to joining the European Parliament in Brussels, Mangiante claims that she worked in New York as an Associate at the global law firm Mayer Brown. In response to this reporter asking Mangiante to confirm that she worked for Mayer Brown in 2007–2008, she said, "Yes. I was a summer associate in Washington for Mayer and Brown, on [sic] 2007. . . . Than [sic] I went to New York where I worked for the same law firm (I was junior associate)."

John D. Tuerck, a firm spokesman, categorically denied that Mangiante has ever worked at Mayer Brown.

"We have no record indicating that someone named Simona Mangiante has worked at Mayer Brown," he said.

When asked if that statement included the position of Junior Associate, Tuerck said, "Our records indicate she was never employed at Mayer Brown, in any capacity."

In an apparent effort to rebuke Tuerck, Mangiante posted a letter on Twitter purporting to be from John P. Schmitz, a former partner of Mayer Brown. The letter appears to be an offer of an internship from Mayer Brown to Mangiante. She did not address how this letter supported her claims that she was a licensed Associate with the law firm. The Mayer Brown spokesman maintained that they had no records that Mangiante was ever employed at the firm, and that the HR department had "checked carefully." Schmitz's new law firm did not immediately respond to a request for comment.

Revisiting Mangiante's LinkedIn also reveals an educational timeline that appears to make little sense. According to the Law Society of England and Wales, to be able to practice law in Italy, one must "complete a five-year law course at an Italian University and a traineeship of at least eighteen months at an Italian law firm." In addition to these six-and-a-half years, the prospective lawyer has to pass the country's bar exam.

Mangiante claims that she only attended school in Italy for four years total, which would make it implausible for her to be a licensed lawyer. A search of the last name "Mangiante" in a database of eligible lawyers in Rome and Milan shows no results. According to her LinkedIn page, Mangiante lists Rome as a location for her current "international law and government advocacy." This search doesn't appear to be comprehensive for the entirety of Italy, meaning Mangiante may be able to practice law in a different part of the country.

A search of the Naples Bar Association confirms that Mangiante is registered to practice law there as of late 2010. Thus, unless registered elsewhere, her educational timeline and practice as an associate prior to 2010 appear to be misleading.

Requests for records and comments to three of Mangiante's listed universities went unanswered as of the time of this publication. New York University, where Mangiante says she participated in an exchange program, said that records of exchange students are confidential.

Concerned family and friends

Family members and friends of the former Trump adviser George Papadopoulos say that his new wife has been misleading about her age, employment history, and details about her activities in 2016.

Over a period of two weeks in late September and October, two family members and a former colleague of Mangiante informed me of their concerns about Mangiante's truthfulness with the public about her background. All three spoke on condition of anonymity because of the sensitivity of the topic.

Legal documents described to me by two sources allege that Mangiante is not thirty years old, as described in an article earlier this year, nor thirty-four, as depicted in a European Parliament biography, but rather thirty-seven, with a birth month of January 1981. One of the sources claimed that after repeated questioning by family members, Mangiante admitted her true age of thirty-seven.

When asked for comment about these inconsistencies in her age, Mangiante said, "I share my passport details and birth certificate for legitimate purposes and not to feed anyone's curiosity. I don't care if people say I am 20 or 40."

The two family members told me that Mangiante told friends and family that she lived in a small one-bedroom condo in South Kensington during her time in London in 2016, partially corroborated by a story in the *Guardian*.

However, domain registration details for a website set up by Mangiante in October, 2016 show that her listed address was not a one-bedroom condo in South Kensington, but rather a two-bedroom, $1.5M flat in the Hampstead area of North London. It is unclear if Mangiante was actually residing at this address or if she listed an address other than her own. After originally stating that she stayed at one address, Mangiante later corrected the record, stating that she indeed had three addresses in London.

The owner of the flat appears to have no connection to Mangiante, and all available evidence points to the idea that she rented the property, which would've fallen at approximately $4,500 per month, according to the UK property company Zoopla. Mangiante claims that she was never paid for her work in London, which happened to be for Professor Mifsud.

When asked how she supported herself in London, Mangiante said, "I am an attorney and I have been working on cases of child abductions as my own practice. I am also the spokeswoman for an association of parents in Europe and this Brought to me a lot of work (while I was based in London)."

An archived version of the now-deleted website for "International Child Abduction Slovakia" shows that Mangiante was indeed the spokeswoman, though the website wasn't registered until October 2016, after Mangiante had already been in London.

The purported background of Simona Mangiante is deceptive at best. The years leading up to her involvement with the European Parliament appear to have been falsified or greatly exaggerated.

Peter Carr, a spokesman for the Special Counsel's office, declined to comment on Mangiante. She has not been charged or accused of any wrongdoing.

Subsequent Information

The strange story of Mr. and Mrs. Papadopoulos continues to evolve by the day. In an effort to push back against my reporting, Mrs. Papadopoulos showed a picture of her passport to ABC News to confirm her true age of thirty-four. Five days after the ABC report, I exclusively obtained a copy of the Papadopoulos's marriage certificate. The listed age of Mrs. Papadopoulos? Thirty-seven.

After sharing this news on Twitter, I was stunned to see Mrs. Papadopoulos admit that she doctored the image of her passport that she showed to ABC to make herself appear three years younger. "[T]he picture of my passport was photoshopped to provoke journalist," she said. Her excuse was that it was a joke, a flippant attempt for the sake of vanity.

As Jeb Bush would say: Please clap.

After being sentenced to fourteen days in prison, a very light sentence by all accounts, Mr. Papadopoulos threatened to tear up his plea deal, spreading the conspiracy theory that he was entrapped by the FBI. Without any proof, he repeatedly claimed that Mr. Mifsud was a western intelligence asset whose real job was to infiltrate the Trump campaign. His wife echoed his sentiments.

I began to investigate Mr. Mifsud's lawyer and alleged "funder," a multi-millionaire Swiss man by the name of Stephan Roh. Many of Mr. Roh's statements declaring that his client Mr. Mifsud was working for the FBI in order to entrap Mr. Papadopoulos struck me as incredibly odd. Both Mr. and Mrs. Papadopoulos cited Mr. Roh's declarations as proof for their conspiracy theories.

"I get indicted for a meeting with a western intelligence asset, Joseph Mifsud, masquerading as a Russian middleman whose own lawyer says was working for the FBI. What a waste of time and money" Mr. Papadopoulos tweeted in December 2018.

Mr. Roh's business empire relied on Russian commerce, my research found. He managed and owned multiple Cyprus-based investment funds and companies that invested exclusively in Russia. At least one of the funds dealt with Russian government bonds and securities. Mr. Roh also managed the assets of some of the most powerful Russian oligarchs, including billionaire Gleb Fetisov.

R& B RUSSIA INVESTMENT FUND LIMITED	Date and type of recognition by the Central Bank of Cyprus: 6/11/2003
	International variable capital company designated as a private ICIS
	Number of Recognition: IBFSS/ICIS 16/30990
	Registered Address: 15 Nafpliou Street, 2nd Floor, 3025 Lemesos.
	Objective of the scheme :
	Maximise profits by investing in a portfolio of fixed income Russian securities, government bonds and money market instruments
	DIRECTORS OF ICIS:
	Name: Mr Stephan Roh **Nationality:** Swiss
	Name: Pambos Papas **Nationality:** Cypriot

Mr. Roh's mother-in-law, Svetlana Vassylyevna, was the head of Intourist for the famous Moscow Metropol hotel until 1992. Intourist handled all of the travels of famous foreigners in the USSR. It is now widely believed to have been just a front for the KGB. Olga Roh, Stephan's Russian wife, wrote about her mother in 2016, confirming the details about Intourist. Olga "grew up" in the Metropol hotel and mingled with KGB-affiliated people.

These connections to Russian billionaires, intelligence agencies, and the mysterious Maltese professor, Joseph Mifsud, eventually landed Mr. Roh under the microscope of Mr. Mueller's investigators. In late 2017, Mr. Roh was stopped by FBI agents in New York and questioned for hours by a small group of investigators.

In the midst of my research and reporting on Mr. Roh's various ties to Russian movers-and-shakers, I received an email from the Swiss lawyer, demanding that I stop my "false and defamatory allegations" against Joseph Mifsud.

Dear Mr Stedman

May I contact you, as my team made me aware of some of your public Twitter messages.

RoH Attorneys at law represents the interests of Prof Joseph Mifsud. We have been mandated recently.

Prof Mifsud instructed us to intervene when false and defamatory allegations are published about him: Please receive this email as a formal cease and desist notice/letter.

It appears and can be understood that you state in your Twitter messages that Prof Mifsud is a Russian agent (asset, cut-out, representative etc.) who has discussed with and offered to Mr Papadopoulos "emails with dirt on Hillary Clinton". Prof Mifsud, initially and further denies and opposes to such narrative: Prof Mifsud never discussed (or offered) such emails, as well he condemns strongly any accusation him being a Russian agent etc.

You are requested to cease and desist from aforementioned false public and defamatory statements. The majority of the media has now accepted the evidence and fact that Prof Mifsud is a Western intelligence operative - and that he has been made available by Western intelligence to connect Mr Papadopoulos to one Russian person. Today, same Western intelligence was guiding him to stay quite.

RoH Attorneys are as well instructed to respond to press inquiries and you may address your questions (by email) to us.

Regards,

Dr. Stephan C. Roh

With all of this information coming to light, it remained incredibly suspicious that Mr. and Mrs. Papadopoulos continued to cite Mr. Roh as a truth-teller in the Russia investigation. He was not an objective party, but rather a Russian-backed businessman who had a clear incentive to muddy the waters.

Back on the trail of Mrs. Papadopoulos, I continued to receive intelligence from my source Alex and other relatives. Most of it was unverifiable, including rumors of a mysterious $250,000 payment to Mrs. Papadopoulos sometime in 2016. Alex was privy to a conversation in which Mrs. Papadopoulos claimed that the European Parliament paid her that quarter of a million dollars as part of her contract expiring. Such a payment would be highly irregular. Other information garnered from conversations with Alex proved to be fruitful.

Throughout the entire process of reporting on Mrs. Papadopoulos, I was contacted by powerful people from all walks of life—law enforcement, prominent conservative journalists, lawyers, and others with a simple message: Mrs. Papadopoulos deserved greater scrutiny and they were glad that I had put her under the microscope, so to speak. Many of those who reached out had their own experience with Mrs. Papadopoulos that caused them to be suspicious of her true intentions.

The best indicator that I was truly onto something important, however, was Mrs. Papadopoulos's own actions. As I continued to investigate both Mr. and Mrs. Papadopoulos, the attacks on me increased in frequency and severity. Mrs. Papadopoulos threatened to sue me for defamation and slander (nothing I published was false), but legal papers never arrived. A lawsuit would only further expose the efforts by Mrs. Papadopoulos to mislead the public, a process I would welcome with open arms.

Mrs. Papadopoulos was reported to ICE in late October by people close to Mr. Papadopoulos, who alleged that she broke multiple immigration laws. Among their concerns was the allegation that she was taking money from news organizations for interviews without possessing a work permit. Fox News would later confirm to me that they paid for at least part of Mrs. Papadopoulos's travel and lodging expenses.

As of October 28th, Mr. Papadopoulos announced that "certain elements of the US government have paused her visa to work in this country. An attempt to silence a victim." By this time, Mrs. Papadopoulos resorted to ad-hominem attacks, hurling insults about my age, appearance, and lifestyle. One back-and-forth with the thirty-seven-year-old resulted in her asking me, "do you take drugs?"

In a tweet, she wrote, "I never lied about my work history. I never lived in London without an income. I was a lawyer in London Scott! In international child abductions. Was working at the time on 7 cases, one of them discussed on tv! Scott Stedman is a fraud! Payed to discredit me. What a loser"

Another tweet said, "Scott Stedman ask to my mother in law why she refused to meet your "source" for over 2 years? Dig little Scotty dig . . . (white trash from England to America, still white trash)"

Less frivolous messages were retweeted and liked by Mrs. Papadopoulos: "I'd run & hide if I were you, as you're really pissing me off," one tweet read. Another said, "[b]lock him Simona. He supports the killing of Jews."

Mrs. Papadopoulos continued to block and unblock my accounts, sometimes posting dozens of messages about myself and my reporting in a single day. I stand by every word that was written, and have confidence that the full story of Mrs. Papadopoulos will be revealed soon.

Late in 2018, as Mr. Papadopoulos was preparing to report to federal prison for lying to the FBI, I was able to obtain a letter sent to Congressman Adam Schiff by a person who represented themselves as someone close to Mr. Papadopoulos during late 2016 and early 2017. The letter made a series of eye-opening claims that thrust Mr. Papadopoulos back in the crosshairs of Congressional and federal investigators. The claims made by the Papadopoulos confidant were as follows:

> Mr. Papadopoulos was working on a Russian business deal with the knowledge of Mr. Trump that would "set him up for life."
>
> The source overheard a phone call between Mr. Trump and Mr. Papadopoulos in December 2016.
>
> Greek and Russian Orthodox leaders were playing "an important role" in the secret effort by the Trump team to collaborate with Russians.

I pretty quickly realized that this incredible document needed to be provided to a journalist with more reach and impact than myself. I decided to share the premise of the story with Natasha Bertrand, a journalist for whom I have a tremendous amount of respect and admiration. Her strong reaction only confirmed to me that this story was important and worth pursuing.

Utilizing the combination of our portfolio of sources, Natasha and I produced and published a report in the *Atlantic* on the letter and the fact that our sources from Congress and the FBI were taking the claims very seriously.

The FBI found the letter so intriguing that they reached out to the person who sent the document to Mr. Schiff and promptly requested an in-person interview to assess the veracity of the claims.

Abstract

Though Mr. Papadopoulos was the first person arrested in connection to Mr. Mueller's investigation into possible coordination between the

Trump campaign and the Russian government, questions about his 2016 activities linger.

Immediately after his arrest was made public, senior members of Mr. Trump's team began spreading egregious disinformation trying to diminish the role that Mr. Papadopoulos played on the campaign. My articles on Mr. Papadopoulos proved that not only did he meet foreign leaders around the world on behalf of the Trump campaign, but that those leaders had connections to Russian entities that were involved in the cyber attack on the United States in 2016.

Following the surprise election of Mr. Trump, Mr. Papadopoulos met an Italian woman who also happened to work for Mr. Mifsud, and the two soon traveled throughout Europe and got married in early 2018. Mrs. Papadopoulos, who was interviewed by the FBI when she arrived in the United States, seemed to change her opinion of the Russia investigation abruptly. First declaring that her new husband would be remembered as a John Dean figure who fully cooperated with authorities, Mrs. Papadopoulos suddenly began blaming the FBI, CIA, and other American agencies for "entrapping" her husband.

Finding this sudden change of heart suspicious, I probed Mrs. Papadopoulos's alleged professional background and discovered that she may not be who she says she is.

Russian Infiltration of the National Rifle Association

Who's Who:
- **Alexander Torshin:** Mafia-connected Russian politician and banker.
- **Maria Butina:** Young Russian assistant to Mr. Torshin
- **Paul Erickson:** Republican operative who advised many GOP campaigns.
- **David Keene:** Former President of the NRA.
- **John Bolton:** Former Ambassador to the UN under George Bush, current Trump National Security Adviser.

Overview

Perhaps one of the most successful infiltration operations of an American political movement by a foreign government in modern history was carried out in the past decade by a well-known Moscow banker and his young, red-headed female sidekick. It sounds like the plotline to a cheesy Hollywood movie, but it happened, and the full scope of their activities is yet to be revealed.

The efforts of the Russian banker and politician, Alexander Torshin, and his twenty-something protégée, Maria Butina, date back to at least 2009, when Mr. Torshin attempted to meet Sarah Palin during his first trip to the United States. Mrs. Palin declined the offer, instead sending her lieutenant to meet with Mr. Torshin, where they discussed gun rights, among other topics.

Over the next two years, Mr. Torshin would hold meetings with various members of the conservative movement, including then-president of the NRA David Keene, Dr. Edward Lozansky, Nashville lawyer G. Kline Preston, and others. While this process of courtship was taking place in America, a twenty-three-year-old furniture saleswoman from Siberia named Maria Butina created a pro-gun political movement in Russia and named her organization "Right to Bear Arms."

Right to Bear Arms was established with the support of Mr. Torshin in late 2011. Though it remains unclear how Ms. Butina first met Mr. Torshin, who is thirty-five years her senior, it appears to have stemmed from volunteer work that she did for the youth wing of the United Russia party, of which Mr. Torshin was a prominent member. The two became partners in crime, literally and figuratively, travelling to the United States often to advance the interests of the Russian Federation.

In mid-2013, the Spanish Civil Guard, which had been monitoring Mr. Torshin's money flows in and out of Spain, confidentially concluded that the Moscow-based politician was one of the most influential members of the Tambovskaya mafia in Russia. They linked many of Mr. Torshin's financial transactions to money-laundering schemes through various banking institutions and real estate properties in Spain. Over a series of dozens of wiretapped conversations, members of the Tambovskaya gang can be heard referring to Mr. Torshin as the "godfather" of the crime group. These members, according to Spanish police, are on tape saying that they conducted money laundering operations at the behest of Mr. Torshin. Spanish authorities prepared an intricate and delicate plan to arrest Mr. Torshin during one of his planned trips to Mallorca, but he mysteriously cancelled his trip at the last minute, and he has not been seen in Spain since.

His activities with Maria Butina in the United States, however, continued without interruption. The two attended nearly every annual NRA convention, where they continued to build and strengthen their relationships with gun activists. Late in 2013, Right to Bear Arms held their annual meeting in Moscow, but something was different this time. American leaders, including Mr. Keene, Alan Gottlieb, president of the Second Amendment Foundation, and GOP operative Paul Erickson showed up. The presence of these American figures established a sense of credibility for Right to Bear Arms, and soon its membership numbers dramatically increased. Ms. Butina took a particular interest in Mr. Erickson, who was very well-connected to Republican leaders from his time on various presidential campaigns.

Ms. Butina and Mr. Erickson, who is twenty-six years older than Ms. Butina, appeared at numerous gun-rights events together and soon began a romantic relationship as well. They traveled back and forth between Moscow, Washington DC, and South Dakota, where Mr. Erickson lived and worked as a lawyer. Ms. Butina visited the NRA headquarters, continued to attend NRA conventions with Mr. Torshin, and published various op-eds in support of gun rights in America and Russia.

In 2015, though, the goals of Ms. Butina and Mr. Torshin appeared to change fairly dramatically. While still showing interest in gun rights causes, Ms. Butina began to leverage the contacts in the Republican party that she and Mr. Torshin had developed over the past six-plus years. Her attention turned much more political, acting as a liaison between the Russian government and Republicans in the United States.

In an email sent by Ms. Butina to Mr. Erickson in early 2015, obtained by prosecutors, she stated that the Republican party, "would likely obtain control over the U.S. government after the 2016 elections."

The Republican party, however, is "traditionally associated with negative and aggressive foreign policy, particularly with regards to Russia," Ms. Butina wrote. "However, now with the right to negotiate seems best to build konstruktivnyh [sic] relations;"

Ms. Butina would go on to note in broken English the "central place and influence in the Republican party plays the NRA. The NRA [is] the largest sponsor of the elections to the US congress."

Thus, Ms. Butina was, for the first time, attempting to cultivate her sources in the NRA to improve relations between the United States government and the Russian government. She regularly checked in with Mr. Torshin, who for all intents and purposes was acting as her handler by this point.

In Las Vegas in mid-2015, Ms. Butina appeared at the FreedomFest, a gathering of libertarians and other right-leaning politicos. Among the speakers at the event was then-candidate Trump, who happened to call on Ms. Butina, who was ready with a question about sanctions on the Russian government.

"I'm from Russia. My question will be about foreign politics," Butina said. "If you will be elected as president, what will be your foreign politics, especially in the relationships with my country? Do you want to continue the policy of sanctions that are damaging both economies? Or have any other ideas?"

"I know Putin, and I'll tell you what, we'll get along with Putin," Mr. Trump responded. "I would get along very nicely with Putin, I mean, where we have the strength. I don't think you'd need the sanctions. I think we would get along very, very well."

Advisers of Mr. Trump would later admit to finding this incident strange. It didn't make much sense that Mr. Trump knew to call on someone who was likely the only Russian in the crowd of thousands, never mind the fact that Mr. Trump had an answer ready to go without even letting Ms. Butina finish her question. At this point in the campaign, Mr. Trump didn't have many policy proposals, especially when it came to foreign policy, so how did he have a fully formed position on the topic of Russian sanctions? Reince Priebus and Steve Bannon reportedly wondered.

At any rate, in December 2015, Mr. Torshin and Ms. Butina coordinated plans to invite leaders of the NRA to a conference in Moscow in an effort to conduct "a serious mission—restoration of relations between countries."

The NRA delegation included Mr. Keene, now-president of the NRA Pete Brownell, Sheriff David Clarke, and Mr. Erickson. They met with Mr. Torshin and Russian Deputy Prime Minister Dmitry Rogozin, who had recently been sanctioned by the Obama administration. Their trip coincidentally overlapped with a visit to Moscow by Trump adviser Michael Flynn and Green Party candidate Jill Stein, who attended a dinner in support of the television network Russia Today. The two American political leaders sat at the same small dinner table as Mr. Putin.

Over a period of five days, the NRA delegation paraded around

Moscow meeting Russian government officials, business leaders, and others. Mr. Clarke tweeted a picture of himself standing with a Russian military member on December 10th, saying, "Red Square near the Kremlin with a Russian officer. Met earlier with Russian Foreign Minister."

Mr. Torshin and Ms. Butina reportedly threw two parties for the NRA leaders, wherein the men and women wined and dined with their Russian associates. "They were killing us with vodka and the best Russian food," one of the NRA attendees said. "The trip exceeded my expectations by logarithmic levels."

Back in the United States in early 2016, Ms. Butina continued to update Mr. Torshin on her political activities. By this point, the two Russians were fully taking advantage of their long-standing relationships with political leaders; Mr. Torshin and Ms. Butina arranged to attend the National Prayer Breakfast in Washington DC in February, and they did so.

Later that month, Ms. Butina and Mr. Erickson incorporated a bizarre shell company in South Dakota, "Bridges LLC." This company caught the attention of federal authorities, and they have since probed the various flows of money in and out of the LLC. Mr. Erickson later told the press that the company was formed in case Ms. Butina needed any monetary assistance for her graduate studies—"an unusual way to use an LLC," one media report noted.

In a March 10th email to a US friend involved in arranging potential meetings between Ms. Butina, Mr. Torshin, and conservative leaders, Ms. Butina wrote, "Torshin was very much impressed by you and expresses his great appreciation for what you are doing to restore relations between the two countries. He also wants you to know that Russians will support the efforts from our side."

By May, Mr. Erickson was reaching out directly to the Trump campaign. He sent an email to campaign adviser Rick Dearborn, titled "Kremlin Connection."

I'm now writing to you and Sen. Sessions in your roles as Trump foreign policy experts / advisors. [. . .] Happenstance and the (sometimes) international reach of the NRA placed me in a position a couple of years ago to slowly begin cultivating a back-channel to President Putin's Kremlin. Russia is quietly but actively seeking a dialogue with the U.S. that isn't forthcoming under the current administration. And for reasons that we can discuss in person or on the phone, the Kremlin believes that the only possibility of a true re-set in this relationship would be with a new Republican White House.

The email would go on to say that Russia hoped to make "first contact" with someone from the Trump team during the upcoming NRA convention. "Putin is deadly serious about building a good relationship with Mr. Trump," Mr. Erickson wrote. "He wants to extend an invitation to Mr. Trump to visit him in the Kremlin before the election."

At the NRA convention previously mentioned, Ms. Butina and Mr. Torshin managed to have a short conversation with the candidate's son, Donald Trump Jr. The first contact had been made. It is uncertain if Ms. Butina or Mr. Torshin raised the prospects of improved US–Russian relations, though both sides deny it. Ms. Butina was even able to snap a photo of herself with NRA President Mr. Brownell and Mr. Trump Jr.

After the Russian hack of the Democratic National Committee was made public in July, Mr. Torshin, Mr. Erickson, and Ms. Butina exchanged a series of messages with concerns that the hack might affect their "covert influence operation." The three continued to communicate throughout 2016 and made repeated references to the secret back-channel of communications between the Kremlin and the Trump campaign that they had created.

Ms. Butina, while still in a relationship with Mr. Erickson, went on a date with another Trump adviser, J. D. Gordon, in October. The two took time out of their schedules just three weeks before the election to attend a Styx concert in Washington, DC. The full extent of the relationship between Mr. Gordon and Ms. Butina remains cloudy.

On election night, Ms. Butina and Mr. Torshin sent messages back-and-forth celebrating. "I am ready for further orders," Ms. Butina wrote, all but confirming her status as an asset of the Russian government under the guidance of Mr. Torshin.

After the surprise election of Mr. Trump, Ms. Butina and Mr. Torshin further exchanged Twitter messages that nearly totally corroborate one of the memos drafted by the ex-British spy, Mr. Steele. According to Mr. Steele, the Kremlin had intervened to block Mitt Romney from becoming Secretary of State. The memo said that the Kremlin had asked Trump to appoint someone who would be prepared to lift Ukraine-related sanctions, and who would cooperate on security issues of interest to Russia, according to a report in the *New Yorker*.

Federal prosecutors later revealed that Ms. Butina and Mr. Torshin were indeed discussing Mr. Trump's impending selection of the Secretary of State.

"After speculating about who might be nominated as Secretary of State, BUTINA suggested a phone call to discuss, and [Torshin] noted that he liked the idea, but was worried that 'all our phones are being listened to!'" according to the FBI. "BUTINA suggested that they talk via WhatsApp. On November 11, 2016, BUTINA sent [Torshin] a direct message via Twitter, in which she predicted who might be named Secretary of State and asked the [Torshin] to find out how 'our people' felt about that potential nomination."

This incredible tick-tock of how the Russian government infiltrated the conservative movement in America, and later the Trump campaign and transition, resulted in criminal charges against Ms. Butina. Federal authorities charged her with acting as a secret foreign agent of the Russian government, for which, as of late 2018, she currently awaits trial. Investigators continue to examine Mr. Erickson's activities as they consider further charges stemming from the secret effort to aid the Kremlin in their effort to boost Mr. Trump and influence American foreign policy.

My contribution to the NRA-Russia story was threefold: First, I established the long-standing relationship between Mr. Torshin and Mr. Keene in the form of a handwritten letter that I was able to exclusively acquire. I then found a curious connection between Mr. Trump's National Security Adviser John Bolton and Right To Bear

Arms. Finally, I proved that Ms. Butina was supported by the Kremlin based on leaked Russian text messages, well before prosecutors officially brought charges against Ms. Butina.

The Process

My first story on the NRA relied heavily on human sources. Unfortunately, this means that I cannot divulge much about the process of obtaining the following information.

My sources for the report requested anonymity because of the sensitivity of the material disclosed. Leaking documents, especially when an alleged Russian mafia-connected politician is involved, can put sources in real danger. The safety of these sources is paramount and never something that I would compromise in any way.

February 20, 2018
In 2011 Handwritten Letter, NRA President Offered Help to Alexander Torshin for His "Endeavors"

The note, dated May 7th, 2011, included a promise of a formal invitation to the NRA's annual convention

Former NRA President David Keene wrote a personal letter to Russian Senator Alexander Torshin in 2011 offering the NRA's help for Torshin's endeavors. The handwritten note was inscribed on official NRA letterhead days after Torshin attended his first NRA convention in Pittsburgh, Pennsylvania.

> Dear Sen. Torshin,
> Just a brief note to let you know just how much I enjoyed our meeting in Pittsburgh during the NRA annual meeting.
> As I indicated, you and your colleagues will receive a formal

invitation to next year's meeting in St. Louis. For planning purposes, you may wish to note that it will be held on April 12–17th, 2012.

In the interim, if there is anything any of us can do to help you in your endeavors, then, please don't hesitate to let us know.

With all best wishes . . . David Keene

It is unclear to what endeavors Keene was referring. Right To Bear Arms, a pro-gun Russian group headed by Torshin's deputy Maria Butina, was not founded until fifteen months after the letter was written. A source with knowledge of the conversations between Keene and Torshin indicated that financial support from the NRA to Torshin was discussed. It is not known whether money ever changed hands. Keene and Torshin did not immediately return requests for comment, and Torshin blocked me on Twitter.

Special Counsel Robert Mueller is investigating Torshin and whether any Russian money went to the NRA to help Trump. During the campaign, Torshin attempted to broker a backdoor line of communication between candidate Trump and Vladimir Putin.

Peter Carr, a spokesman for Mueller's office, declined to comment on Tuesday.

The disclosure of the letter from Keene to Torshin is the first piece of evidence that the NRA directly offered assistance to the Kremlin ally. The NRA has attempted to downplay their relationship with Torshin, noting that they have not been contacted by anyone in the FBI regarding the Russia probe. One month after receiving the letter, Torshin was pictured alongside Vladimir Putin in Moscow.

Torshin's colorful history has been the subject of intense media scrutiny in recent months. Connections to a money laundering operation in Spain and the Russian mafia have emerged.

According to a confidential report by the Spanish Civil Guard, Torshin allegedly, "instructed members of the Moscow-based Taganskaya crime syndicate how to launder ill-gotten gains through banks and properties in Spain while he was a deputy speaker of the upper house of parliament." The Russian politician was known as the leader of the crime syndicate, and was often referred to as the "godfather" of the group. The NRA letter arrived amidst his reported illegal activities.

In 2015, Torshin was nominated as a deputy head of the Central Bank of Russia—a position that gives him access to Putin like few others in the Russian government. The Senator-turned-banker has had multiple meetings with those in Trump's orbit, both prior to and during the campaign.

Torshin was photographed in a December 2015 Moscow meeting with Sheriff David Clarke, NRA leader Pete Brownell, and Russian Deputy Prime Minister Dmitry Rogozin, among others. The trip to Russia was organized by Butina's The Right To Bear Arms.

At the 2016 NRA convention, Trump Jr. met with Torshin. According to Trump Jr.'s lawyer Alan Futerfas, the two "made small talk for a few minutes and went back to their separate meals."

The revelation of the note sent by Keene to one of Putin's closest allies raises new questions about the relationship between the NRA and the Kremlin. It portrays a willingness to develop an operational alliance. According to the Center for Responsive Politics, NRA spending surged by $100 million in 2016 compared to previous election cycles. As a 501c(4) non-profit, the NRA does not have to disclose its donors.

"No politician benefited more from the NRA's 2016 spending binge than President Donald Trump," the Center for Responsive Politics report concluded. "The NRA spent over $30 million in support of Trump's candidacy—or more than its combined spending in all races during the 2008 and 2012 presidential election cycles."

Under 52 U.S. Code § 30121, it is a federal crime for a foreign national to make a contribution or donation of money or other thing of value to influence an election cycle. Robert Mueller's probe into the NRA's connections to the Kremlin is ongoing.

With Ms. Butina under increasing scrutiny by federal authorities and investigative journalists, I turned my attention to the years leading up to her involvement with the 2016 campaign. Major media reports had scoured her Facebook and the Facebook page of her organization, Right To Bear Arms, but seemed to end their hunt there.

In Russia, Facebook isn't as popular as other social media networking sites such as VKontakte (VK) or OK.ru. My inclination was to dig deeper than just the Facebook and Twitter pages of Ms. Butina and expand my search to the aforementioned Russian social media platforms. On VK, I searched Maria Butina in Russian—"Мария Бутина"—and quickly found her profile there with many more posts and photos than were included on her Facebook page.

From there, I located the VK page for Right to Bear Arms and began combing through the photos and videos posted by the Moscow-based organization. Scrolling through the hundreds of pictures, events, and videos proved to be tedious and fruitless until I discovered a familiar face.

John Bolton, who was at the time of my research into Ms. Butina being rumored to replace H. R. McMaster as National Security Adviser, appeared on a screen before a large group of Russians, including Ms. Butina. To determine why Mr. Bolton made a video appearance at a meeting for Right To Bear Arms, I ran a reverse image search of the picture from the VK page.

The reverse image search, which sifts through all available web pages to find an exact match, showed that the image was used on an online journal written by Ms. Butina. Her post, which included video of Mr. Bolton's three-minute speech, became the foundation of my next report on Ms. Butina and her organization's ties to leading Republican figures.

March 20, 2018

John Bolton Spoke at 2013 Round-Table for Russian Gun-Rights Group Under Scrutiny in Mueller Investigation

The rumored pick for Trump's next National Security Adviser, John Bolton, made a guest appearance at a 2013 round-table organized by Right to Bear Arms in Russia, a group whose leaders are under investigation by Special Counsel Robert Mueller.

The video appearance by the former Ambassador to the United Nations included an ardent support of the Second Amendment and the hope that Russia will adopt similar legislation. "We pray for you to preserve these first precious freedoms," Bolton said. The group of Russians to whom Bolton spoke included State Duma members as well as leaders of Butina's organization.

"One of the leading neocons in the US, speaking with the wishes of positive changes in Russia and going for a dialogue, is great and is a huge success of our people," Butina wrote on her personal blog, highlighting the speech by Bolton as an important sign of cooperation between her gun advocacy group and political leaders in the United States.

The newly discovered speech by Bolton comes at a time when he is being considered to become President Trump's National Security Adviser (NSA) following the likely sacking of current NSA General H.R. McMaster. Bolton has been widely viewed as being at the top of the president's short list for the senior aide position. The sixty-nine-year-old Bolton did not respond to requests for comment.

The leaders of The Right to Bear Arms are Maria Butina and Alexander Torshin—a Putin-allied Russian politician. Both have garnered scrutiny from Congressional investigators and Special Counsel Robert Mueller over a series of suspicious interactions with the Trump campaign and outside groups that funded pro-Trump Super PACs.

Torshin, the deputy head of the Central Bank of Russia and alleged mafia boss, has been cultivating relationships with the NRA and other gun-rights groups in the United States since 2011. He meticulously documented his various excursions with NRA leaders and activists on social media.

In a 2011 handwritten letter, then-President of the NRA David Keene offered help to Alexander Torshin for his "endeavors."

In December 2015, a delegation from the NRA, including Presidents Keene and Pete Brownell, Sheriff David Clarke, and others, flew to Moscow and had a series of meetings with Torshin and other Russian leaders, including Deputy Prime Minister Dmitry Rogozin.

Butina has been Torshin's deputy for years, often accompanying him on his trips to the United States. She, however, has been more aggressive in pushing her pro-gun agenda internationally as the leader of The Right to Bear Arms.

Her appearance at one of then-candidate Trump's first official events in July 2015 raised eyebrows when she asked a question about easing Russian sanctions after being selected by Trump. The newly declared candidate responded by saying, "I don't think you'd need the sanctions." Steve Bannon and Reince Priebus reportedly found the encounter puzzling. The two Trump campaign officials found it odd that Trump happened to call on Butina and had a fully formed answer ready when asked about US–Russia relations.

Butina did not respond to multiple requests for comment.

By 2016, the relationship between Republican leaders in the United States and the team of Torshin-Butina were so well established that a Trump-Putin meeting was offered to the campaign by conservative activist Paul Erickson. Erickson wrote, "Putin is deadly serious about building a good relationship with Mr. Trump." Though the meeting never took place, the offer highlighted Torshin's years-long effort to gain influence in the political process of the United States on behalf of Russian leadership.

Butina and Erickson set up a mysterious South Dakota company in February 2016 called Bridges LLC, paying an extra fee to the Secretary of State's office in order to incorporate the company on an expedited timeline. Erickson told McClatchy in 2017 that the company was "established in case Butina needed any monetary assistance for her graduate studies." McClatchy noted that the given reason was a strange way to use an LLC.

The inclusion of Bolton in this tangled web of connections between The Right to Bear Arms in Russia and conservative leaders in the United States raises new questions about his suitability to become National Security Adviser.

In his public statements, Bolton has offered conflicting views on the Russian interference in the 2016 US elections. He has been tough on Russian aggression, while at the same time said in a recent op-ed that "there is, to date, no evidence of collusion, express or implied, nor can it honestly be said that Russia was 'pro-Trump.'" In the days after the publication of the Trump dossier, Bolton called those who commissioned the dossier "worse than prostitutes."

The Federal Election Committee and Special Counsel Robert Mueller are investigating whether Russian money went to the NRA to support Trump.

Maria Butina, Alexander Torshin, and their group, Right to Bear Arms, are of interest to the team of Mueller's prosecutors. The extent of Ambassador Bolton's relationship with the group remains unclear.

———————

My final report on Ms. Butina and her relationship with the NRA proved without a shred of doubt that the Kremlin discussed ways in which to support her efforts, something that would, months later, be confirmed by federal prosecutors in the United States.

Leaked messages from inside Mr. Putin's presidential staff first popped up on my radar when researching Konstantin Rykov, a Kremlin propagandist who is discussed at length later in this book. By now, I had contacted a journalist in Europe who wrote about the leak, and, with the help of a colleague, I was able to obtain the full file of messages.

I wish I had a more interesting story to tell here, but at the time that I was able to get my hands on the messages, I was focused on researching Ms. Butina and her activities, so I simply searched the folder of messages for Butina ("Бутина") and found what I was looking for: concrete evidence that Mr. Putin's staff members had discussions about supporting Ms. Butina as she visited the NRA headquarters in Virginia.

The second part of my April report relied on human sources who provided photographs to me of the events in Moscow attended by the NRA delegation in 2015. To protect the identity of my sources, I am unable to divulge the process by which I acquired these pictures. In this case, I had been talking to my sources for months. The level of trust they had with me to provide such information means that I owe it to them to not characterize their involvement at all.

———————

April 6, 2018
Kremlin Discussed Support for Maria Butina as She Visited NRA Headquarters in 2014

Exclusively obtained photos show Sheriff Clarke and NRA leaders drinking with Russian politicians and Putin confidants in 2015

Leaked 2014 text messages from Kremlin officials have shown that the Russian government was discussing support for the woman whose outreach to NRA members has drawn scrutiny from Special Counsel Robert Mueller.

Maria Butina, a Russian national and deputy to the scandal-plagued Alexander Torshin, has garnered attention from US investigators as they probe whether any Russian money flowed to the NRA in support of then-candidate Trump. The duo's outreach to gun-rights activists in the United States dates back to 2011, when Torshin attended his first NRA convention.

Butina has insisted that her pro-gun group Right to Bear Arms is entirely independent from any Kremlin backing.

"Hey. Help please," reads a May 2014 text message from Marika Korotaeva, a Kremlin official, to her boss, Timur Prokopenko. "Butina (for legalization of weapons) . . . now posts pictures with the President of the US gunsmiths now at the main office in Virginia. Against the background of statements about the supply of arms to Ukraine. I ask your help."

The picture Butina posted on Twitter was accompanied by a caption in Russian that, when translated, read, "With U.S. gunworkers-NRA president David Kein at Virginia's main office". This tweet caught the attention of the Kremlin as it debated whether to support Butina's efforts.

Prokopenko serves as the head of the Internal Politics department in President Putin's administration. A Russian group known as "Humpty Dumpty" released Prokopenko's text messages to various journalists in Europe and elsewhere. These messages were then exclusively shared and verified via open-source information.

It is unclear what action, if any, the Russian government took to support Butina. She could not be reached for comment.

Among the various activities undertaken by Butina that have caught the eye of investigators is the incorporation of a South Dakota company called

"Bridges, LLC" in February, 2016. Records show that the company was established by Butina and conservative activist Paul Erickson. In a phone interview last year with McClatchy, Erickson claimed that the firm was established in case Butina needed any monetary assistance for her graduate studies.

Documents filed with the South Dakota Secretary of State indicate that Butina and Erickson paid an extra fee to have the company's incorporation expedited. It remains unknown why the two found it necessary to hasten the process.

Filing Date:	02/10/2016	
Re:	Bridges, LLC (DL047027) Articles of Organization	

The documents on behalf of Bridges, LLC have been received and filed. Attached is the Certificate along with a receipt for the filing fee of $200.00. Below is a summary of the transaction.

Remitter	Address	Amount Paid
LYNN JACKSON SHULTZ & LEBRUN PC	PO BOX 2700	$200.00
	SIOUX FALLS, SD 57101-2700	
	Total:	$200.00

The NRA has recently insisted that the only money it has taken from any Russians was Torshin's membership dues, which amounted to less than $1,000. Stephen Hart, outside counsel to the NRA, told ABC News, "I know this is difficult but the political arm of the NRA has not ever accepted foreign contributions. That is illegal."

Hart also said, "They cannot disclose what does not exist."

A spokesman for the Special Counsel's office declined to comment on their ongoing investigation.

Nah zda-rovh-yeh!

Newly obtained photos from the NRA delegation's trip to Moscow in December 2015 offer a behind-the-scenes look at the relationship forged by Russian officials and American gun-rights activists in the lead up to the 2016 election.

The images, taken at a party thrown by Russian politician Alexander Torshin at a Moscow hunting club, show American gun-rights leaders, including Sheriff David Clarke, drinking and laughing with the Russians. The American delegation consisted of the aforementioned Clarke, NRA

Presidents Pete Brownell and David Keene, NRA funders Arnold and Hilary Goldschlager, the Outdoor Channel's Jim and Kim Liberatore, and others. Hosting them were Torshin and leading Russian journalist Pavel Gusev, who has not been previously reported as taking part in any of the NRA activities in Moscow.

The presence of Gusev, the head of the Moscow Journalists' Union, is an important new chapter in the relationship between the NRA and Kremlin allies. Gusev was appointed by Vladimir Putin as a "trustee" or trusted confidant for his campaign in the 2018 Russian elections. This appointment is a recognition of Putin's most ardent supporters and people he trusts to appear on television and other campaign events in his place.

According to Ilya Zaslavskiy, the Head of Research at the Free Russia Foundation, a US non-profit, the group of trusted confidants usually consists of around five hundred "cultural figures and celebrities who meet [Putin] and get televised as his supporters." These representatives are trusted by Putin himself and are often rewarded with "various small and not so small privileges after elections," according to Zaslavskiy.

Zaslavskiy noted that Gusev can sometimes be mildly critical of the Kremlin but remains "definitely a pro-regime guy."

At the time of the party with NRA officials, Gusev was the Chairman of the Public Counsel at the Russian Defense Ministry. In his role as Chairman of the public face of the Russian military, Gusev serves directly under Defense Minister Sergey Shoigu. Widely seen as a potential heir to Putin, Shoigu is considered an inner-circle fixture in the Kremlin.

The leaked text messages and the inclusion of a Putin confidant at a party celebrating the NRA's trip to Moscow raises new questions about the Kremlin's involvement in courting the Americans. In his testimony to the House Intelligence Committee, Fusion GPS founder Glenn Simpson made a point to mention Torshin and Butina: "It appears the Russians," Simpson said, "infiltrated the NRA."

Subsequent Information

Ms. Butina was arrested in July 2018 on charges of conspiracy to defraud the United States and acting as a covert agent of a foreign government under a statute that Justice Department lawyers describe as "espionage-lite." She pleaded not guilty to the charges, but soon entered into plea negotiations with the prosecutors in an attempt to lessen her eventual sentence.

A cooperative Ms. Butina would amount to a coup for investigators. Her knowledge of NRA activities and funding, as well the relationships that she forged with Trump campaign and transition members, would be rife with information for prosecutors as they consider charges against other persons.

Media reports indicated that Mr. Erickson was also in serious legal jeopardy, something the FBI strongly indicated in their affidavit of Ms. Butina.

"There is probable cause to believe that BUTINA conspired with one or more persons to violate 18 U.S.C. § 951, in violation of 18 U.S.C. § 371," the FBI wrote. Mr. Erickson is not named in the document, but is referred to as "U.S. Person 1", an often ominous sign for unindicted individuals.

The shell company Bridges LLC continued to intrigue those investigating the Russian infiltration of the NRA. Multiple articles indicated that the FBI was investigating whether any Russian money ended up in the NRA coffers which, if spent on election-related purchases such as TV ads, would be illegal under federal law.

"Bank officials said they couldn't determine the purpose of [Bridges LLC], which was incorporated in South Dakota in February 2016," *BuzzFeed* reported in late July 2018. "Butina was listed as the 'sole signer' on its checking account, but Erickson wrote and signed checks from it."

The suspicious activity regarding Bridges LLC is viewed in a more sinister light when considering the fact that Ms. Butina's handler, Mr. Torshin, is a notorious money-launderer for the Russian mafia, per officials in Spain. If Russia wanted to launder money into the United States for the purposes of aiding the NRA or some other group, Mr. Torshin would know how to do so effectively and surreptitiously.

Abstract

From 2011 through early 2015, Russian operatives Maria Butina and her handler Alexander Torshin infiltrated the National Rifle Association and numerous other Republican leadership circles. They met with NRA leaders, exchanged gifts, attended conventions and, in the case of Ms. Butina, started a romantic relationship with a prominent pro-gun GOP operative. Their goals during this time appeared to be forging a bond between gun rights activists in the United States and Russia to advance their cause. In 2015, however, Ms. Butina and Mr. Torshin pivoted to their true intentions: influencing the United States' political policy towards Russia.

The two managed to not only infiltrate the NRA, but also the Trump campaign, as they saw his candidacy as the best hope for a Russia-friendly presidency. There exists evidence that they were successful, as Christopher Steele referenced, in picking the first Secretary of State under the Trump administration, an incredible feat for the vicious Putin autocracy.

Through my reporting on Ms. Butina and Mr. Torshin's activities in the United States and Russia, it was established that this was an extensive Russian government-directed effort to shape US policy in the favor of Russia's interests. The extent of their success remains to be seen.

Suspicious Business Dealings, Flights, and a Confession in Plain Sight

Who's Who:
- **Konstantin Kilimnik:** Russian intelligence-trained political adviser and strategist.
- **Oleg Deripaska:** One of Russia's most powerful billionaires, on whom Mr. Putin regularly relies.
- **Carter Page:** Former Trump campaign foreign policy adviser.

Overview

Encompassing Mr. Trump's campaign and subsequent election and inauguration were a series of suspicious business deals, mysterious overnight flights from Moscow to New York, and a confession of sorts on social media from one of the Kremlin's chief propagandists.

Among the most dubious advisers that Mr. Trump onboarded in early 2016 were Paul Manafort and Carter Page. Both men had a large portfolio of financial dealings around the globe, with Mr. Page being in the energy business and Mr. Manafort strategizing for political leaders from DC to Kiev.

Both Mr. Page and Mr. Manafort had caught the attention of federal authorities in the United States well before they joined the Trump campaign. Mr. Manafort and his business and political partner Richard Gates represented the pro-Russian former President of Ukraine, Viktor Yanukovych, in the 2000s. The two men created a web of offshore accounts wherein they received payments from dubious political leaders like Mr. Yanukovych. Mr. Manafort and Mr. Gates also had a multimillion dollar relationship with one of the most powerful Russian oligarchs, Oleg Deripaska. Their connections in Ukraine and Russia had authorities in the United States on alert.

Manafort/Kilimnik/Deripaska

Mr. Manafort spent nearly four decades as a political advisor, starting in the United States on Bob Dole's 1980 presidential campaign but eventually branching off to Africa, the Middle East, and Eastern Europe. In the years leading up to joining the Trump campaign, Mr. Manafort worked for Mr. Yanukovych's Party of Regions in Ukraine.

The financial support that Mr. Manafort received from this political consultancy work ended up in various offshore locations, which made the source of his funding difficult to ascertain. The secrecy laws in the countries where Mr. Manafort kept his money allowed him not to declare the ultimate source of the money. Public reporting on his financial profile, including links to organized crime in Eastern Europe, was one of the reasons that Mr. Manafort was forced out of his position on Mr. Trump's campaign in August 2016.

Mr. Manafort's proximity to the Kremlin-backed Mr. Yanukovych allowed him to develop relationships with two Russians who would ultimately play a critical role in the Mueller probe: Oleg Deripaska and a well-known Russian intelligence–trained asset, Konstantin Kilimnik.

Mr. Deripaska is one of the most powerful Russian billionaires not named Vladimir Putin. He is the founder of the second-largest aluminum company in the world, as well as two other multi-billion-dollar Russian energy companies. His network of businesses reaches all corners of the globe, providing him with substantial political power in Russia and elsewhere. Mr. Deripaska's relationship with Mr. Putin has been tumultuous, but by most accounts he remains in close contact with Mr. Putin.

Earning his fortune in the notoriously brutal environment of the violent "aluminum wars" in Russia in the 1990s, Mr. Deripaska has been banned from entering the United States for years as authorities grew concerned about his connections to the Russian mob. In 2012,

Mr. Deripaska publicly admitted to paying criminal gangs to protect himself during the height of the battles over the control of various aluminum factories. He has long sought to lift his restriction from traveling to the United States, but to no avail.

Mr. Manafort's business relationship with Mr. Deripaska dates back at least a decade, when the Russian oligarch hired Mr. Manafort to the tune of $10 million per year to promote Russian interests around the world. For his work in Mr. Yanukovych's government in Ukraine, Mr. Manafort and his aide Konstantin Kilimnik were once again financially supported by Mr. Deripaska.

Originally hired by Mr. Manafort as a translator, Mr. Kilimnik quickly became Mr. Manafort's right-hand-man in Ukrainian politics. Educated at the Military University of the Ministry of Defense of the Russian Federation, Mr. Kilimnik served in the Soviet Army, working alongside Russian intelligence operatives. His proximity to Russian intelligence and Mr. Manafort's activities in Ukraine and elsewhere put Mr. Kilimnik in the good graces of Mr. Deripaska, who regularly paid Mr. Kilimnik to meet Russian businessmen and political leaders.

By the time that Mr. Manafort joined the Trump campaign, his relationship with Mr. Deripaska had turned sour, with the latter filing lawsuits accusing Mr. Manafort of not repaying nearly $20 million in loans. Mr. Manafort took over as Mr. Trump's campaign chairman in June 2016 in an enormously uncomfortable position: deeply in debt to a mafia-linked Russian billionaire on whom Mr. Putin himself regularly relied.

In an effort to get even, Mr. Manafort reached out to his old friend, Mr. Kilimnik, to give Mr. Deripaska private briefings about the Trump campaign. In one email sent to Mr. Kilimnik in early April 2016, Mr. Manafort referred to press reports naming him as a Trump campaign strategist and said, "I assume you have shown our friends my media coverage, right?"

"Absolutely," Mr. Kilimnik responded, "Every article."

"How do we use to get whole?" Mr. Manafort asked. "Has OVD operation seen?" referring to Mr. Deripaska by his initials OVD.

Seeking to leverage his newly rediscovered American political power into a way to get even with the Russian billionaire, Mr. Manafort offered private briefings to Mr. Deripaska in July as Mr. Trump secured the nomination.

"If he needs private briefings we can accommodate," Mr. Manafort wrote to Mr. Kilimnik with the understanding that he would pass the message along to Mr. Deripaska. Later in July, the correspondences between Mr. Manafort and Mr. Kilimnik became extremely cryptic.

"I met today with the guy who gave you your biggest black caviar jar several years ago," Kilimnik wrote. "We spent about 5 hours talking about his story, and I have several important messages from him to you. He asked me to go and brief you on our conversation. I said I have to run it by you first, but in principle I am prepared to do it, provided that he buys me a ticket. It has to do about the future of his country, and is quite interesting. So, if you are not absolutely against the concept, please let me know which dates/places will work, even next week, and I could come and see you."

Investigators believe that "black caviar" is a reference to financial transactions. Mr. Manafort agreed to the meeting and the two men planned to meet in New York on the following Tuesday, August 2nd.

"I need about two hours," Mr. Kilimnik wrote to Mr. Manafort on July 31, "because it is a long caviar story to tell."

Mr. Manafort and Mr. Kilimnik met over cigars in Manhattan on the evening of August 2nd, days after the Russian-intelligence trained political strategist told the Trump campaign manager that he would be delivering messages from Mr. Deripaska. Make no mistake, these messages from Mr. Deripaska represented a line of communication from the Russian government to Mr. Trump's campaign just days after WikiLeaks had released the first batch of emails from the Democratic National Committee, which investigators have concluded were stolen by Russian intelligence operatives. It remains unclear what the men discussed.

Hours after Mr. Manafort and Mr. Kilimnik met in Manhattan, Mr. Deripaska was filmed on his yacht in Norway alongside the Russian Deputy Prime Minister, Sergei Prikhodko. The videos, taken by Mr. Deripaska's alleged mistress, Nastya Rybka, include the men discussing Russian–US relations, fueling speculation that Mr. Deripaska was acting as a conduit between the Trump team and the Russian government.

Mr. Manafort's financial dealings, his August 2016 meeting with Mr. Kilimnik, and the surrounding circumstances comprised my two reports in February and March of 2018.

The Process

Mr. Manafort's financial empire spanned many locations, from the Cayman Islands to Cyprus to Florida. With the experience I had under my belt with Cypriot documents from my research into Trump Tower Moscow, I turned to Mr. Manafort's various shell companies registered on the small Mediterranean island.

One company in particular, Lucicle Consultants Limited, had already been named by Mr. Mueller's prosecutors in their indictment against Mr. Manafort and Mr. Gates as a vehicle for money laundering and tax evasion. The company had also garnered press attention for the loans it had received from Russian and Ukrainian-connected entities. With this intrigue, I wrote to the Cypriot government a request for all documents filed by Lucicle Consultants Limited.

The folder of documents contained twelve PDFs including audited financial statements, something not always required by the government. On page twenty-three of the financial statements was a list of loans received by the company in the years of 2012 and 2013. Four of the five loans had been identified by various media reports. But the fifth loan, which was by far the biggest, had not been disclosed. This loan, exclusively reported by myself, would be identified by Mr. Mueller's prosecutors some three weeks after my article.

February 1, 2018
The Unreported Loan: Paul Manafort Received Seven Million Dollars in Cyprus from Unidentifiable Company
The 2012 loan came from a company with no public records.

Days before Paul Manafort received a loan from mob-connected Ukrainian politician Ivan Fursin, one of Manafort's Cypriot companies received $7 million from a company that doesn't appear to have existed at the time.

Newly obtained financial statements from one of Manafort's shell companies—Lucicle Consultants Limited—show that Manafort received his biggest loan from Telmar Investments Limited. The loan was issued to Manafort in February 2012, during the period of time that he was advising President Yanukovych of Ukraine.

18.5 Loans from related undertakings (Note 14)	2013 US$	2012 US$
Actinet Trading Limited (note i)	311,509	301,459
Olivenia Trading Limited (note ii)	309,307	-
Mistaro Ventures (note iii)	2,432,699	2,363,573
Black Sea View Limited (note iv)	513,192	-
Telmar Investments Limited (note v)	6,943,157	5,413,329
	10,509,864	8,078,361

(v) On 1 February 2012, the Company entered into a loan agreement with Temar Investments Limited (the "Lender"), where it was agreed that the Lender will provide a loan facility to the Company of US$7.000.000. The loan bears an interest of 3%. As at 31 December 2013, the accrued principle amounted to US$6.663.200 (US$5.327.999) and the accrued interest to US$279.957 (2012: US$85.329).

In the Manafort and Rick Gates indictment, Special Counsel Robert Mueller argued that the two men used Lucicle to avoid paying taxes and to purchase lavish items in the United States. Among the purchases made by Manafort using money from Lucicle include three Range Rovers, a Mercedez-Benz, and a $14,000 piece of art. Manafort also sent $1.9 million from Lucicle to a real estate trust in Virginia to purchase his Arlington home.

A *New York Times* report from June 2017 identified Lucicle, months before the Special Counsel's indictment. In the report, the *Times* found that Manafort had been in debt to pro-Russia interests by as much as $17 million before he joined Trump's presidential campaign. One of the companies that transferred money to Lucicle is owned by Ukrainian Party of Regions member of Parliament Ivan Fursin. A *Daily Beast* article in November of 2017 reported that Fursin was a senior member in the Semion Mogilevich criminal organization, citing a fellow at Johns Hopkins-SAIS Center for Transatlantic Relations.

By far the largest expenditure to Manafort was the $7 million from Telmar in 2012—something the *Times* did not mention. It appears that this money was then transferred to Manafort in the United States. Telmar is the only company that loaned Manafort money that was not mentioned by the Special Counsel's office in the October indictment of Manafort and Gates. The omission is especially noteworthy because of the meticulous details in the indictment, listing every Manafort-involved Cypriot monetary transaction over a period of nearly a decade.

An analysis of Telmar Investments Limited (also spelled 'Temar' in the financial documents) reveals that no such company existed in the public domain at the time the loan was executed. According to OpenCorporates, the only companies sharing the same name were in Gibraltar and the United Kingdom. The Gibraltar company was struck off in 2005, and the United Kingdom company was registered at the end of 2017. Similarly named companies either were dissolved before 2012 or were registered well after. It remains unclear who loaned Manafort the $7 million.

In the months leading up to Manafort joining the Trump campaign, his life was in turmoil. He sobbed daily, according to his daughter, following the collapse of President Yanukovych's regime, the collapse of his marriage, and the collapse of his fortune. He owed millions of dollars to oligarchs in Russia and Ukraine—most notably the Kremlin-insider Oleg Deripaska. Desperate to settle his debts and rebuild his damaged image, he reached out to his friends in Washington and was soon on the Trump campaign.

While leading the campaign, Manafort attended the now-infamous June 2016 Trump Tower meeting with Russian officials claiming to have dirt on Hillary Clinton. According to the transcript of the testimony of Glenn Simpson to House Intelligence investigators, Manafort made a cryptic note during the Trump Tower meeting saying, "value in Cyprus as inter." Weeks after the meeting, he would be emailing an offer to Oleg Deripaska to give him private briefings about campaign issues. Given the context of the relationship between Deripaska and Manafort, it appears that this offer was a way for Manafort to get even with his Russian business partner.

The newly discovered loan to Manafort calls into question to whom he was indebted when he became Chair of Donald Trump's campaign. Manafort and Gates are expected to be on trial in September.

Acting on information provided to me by Juha Keskinen, a Twitter friend who tracks flight logs and goes by the handle of @MacFinn44, I next began to connect the dots between a mysterious overnight flight of Mr. Deripaska's private plane from Moscow to Newark, New Jersey, the Manafort/Kilimnik meeting in Manhattan, and the Deripaska/Prikhodko yacht discussions in Norway.

Flight logs reviewed by myself and Mr. Keskinen created a compelling timeline that certainly circumstantially looked like the foundation of a conspiracy between the Trump campaign and Russia: Mr. Deripaska's private jet flew overnight from Moscow to New Jersey, landing on the morning of the "black caviar" meeting between Mr. Manafort and Mr. Kilimnik. It then took off back to Moscow that same night, where it would thirty hours later take Mr. Prikhodko to the yacht in Norway where Mr. Deripaska was waiting.

The *Guardian* would later report that Congressional investigators had reason to believe that Mr. Kilimnik was aboard the private jet for at least one leg of the trip, back to Moscow.

March 6, 2018
Deripaska's Private Jet: Newark-Moscow-Molde for Secret Yacht Meeting

Konstantin Kilimnik, the Ukrainian political consultant who has ties to Russian intelligence, said the two discussed unpaid bills and current news.

As Trump campaign chairman Paul Manafort and his Ukrainian business partner Konstantin Kilimnik met for a private dinner in Manhattan in August 2016, the private jet of the Russian oligarch to whom Manafort owed millions was crossing the Atlantic en route to Newark, New Jersey.

Kilimnik, who has been assessed by Special Counsel Robert Mueller as having ties to Russian intelligence, wrote in an email days prior, "I met today with the guy who gave you your biggest black caviar jar several years ago," in an apparent reference to Deripaska's loans to Manafort. "We spent about 5 hours talking about his story, and I have several important messages from him to you," Kilimnik wrote before setting up an August 2 meeting with the Trump campaign chief.

"I need about two hours," Kilimnik said in the July 31 email, "because it is a long caviar story to tell." Kilimnik did not immediately respond to requests for comment.

In a fifty-two-hour time period beginning on August 2, Deripaska's private jet went from Newark, NJ—minutes from the meeting location of Manafort and Kilimnik—to Moscow to pick up the Russian Deputy PM, to Norway to accommodate the secret yacht meeting where US–Russian relations were discussed.

As the Manafort dinner with Kilimnik was taking place at 666 Fifth Avenue, owned by Jared Kushner, one of three private jets owned by Deripaska (call-sign M-ALAY) was en route to New Jersey from Moscow. It landed mere hours after the dinner concluded and took off back to Moscow the next evening. It is unclear who was aboard the jet and why the flight was chartered. A spokeswoman for Deripaska did not respond to a request for comment.

Kilimnik told the *Washington Post* that the two "discussed unpaid bills and current news," but not the presidential campaign that Manafort was chairing. The next evening, Deripaska's plane took off from Newark en route back to Moscow. It would soon carry one of the most influential Russian political leaders—Deputy Prime Minister Sergei Prikhodko—to secretly take him to the Russian oligarch's private yacht in Norway, where the billionaire was waiting.

According to Alexei Navalny, the Russian opposition leader who first discovered the yacht video on the Instagram of Deripaska's mistress, Nastya Rybka, Deripaska likely flew from his villa in Montenegro to Molde on his other private jet, M-UGIC. Flight logs confirm that this plane flew from Montenegro to Molde on August 5. Almost assuredly, according to Navalny, the Russian Deputy Prime Minister was on the Moscow-Molde M-ALAY flight, hours after it landed from Newark.

The secret yacht meeting uncovered by Navalny was documented by Deripaska's mistress, Nastya Rybka. Rybka was jailed in Thailand for attending a "sex seminar" and remains behind bars for the foreseeable future. She and her associates have asked for political asylum from the United States in exchange for what she claims is evidence of collusion between the Russian government and the Trump team.

Rybka asserts that she and her group have sixteen-plus hours of audio, video, and photographic evidence that would implicate the Russian government. If deported back to Moscow, she fears for her life, telling the *Washington Post*, "I can say something only when I will be in a safe place, sorry, because I am worried about my life."

In an interview with CNN, Rybka said that she "witnessed several meetings in 2016 and 2017 between Deripaska and at least three un-named Americans." It is unclear if any Americans were on the yacht in August 2016, though flight records strongly suggest that it is a possibility.

The newly discovered flight logs of Deripaska's private jet in August 2016 raises new questions not only about his relationship with Trump's campaign manager, but about his role as a possible facilitator between the Russian government and Trump associates.

Carter Page

Mr. Page, a veteran of the US Navy, began his professional career as an investment banker for Merrill Lynch in New York, London, and Moscow in the early 2000s. Many of his professional business dealings were based in Russia. It was from these contacts in the Russian capital that Mr. Page was the subject of a recruitment effort by Russian intelligence operatives in 2013. According to federal court documents, three members of the SVR (The Foreign Intelligence Service of the Russian Federation) covertly courted Mr. Page with the promise of lucrative business deals. There is no evidence that Mr. Page knew that the three men were intelligence officers, and he was never charged with any legal wrongdoing.

Behind the scenes, however, Mr. Page was bragging about his influence on Russian government policy. In an August 2013 letter to Academic Press, Mr. Page wrote, "Over the past half year, I have had the privilege to serve as an informal advisor to the staff of the Kremlin in preparation for their Presidency of the G-20 Summit next month."

It is no surprise, then, that the FBI and other investigatory bodies in the United States and around the world were highly suspicious when Mr. Page and Mr. Manafort joined the Trump campaign within days of one another in March 2016. Though Mr. Manafort held a much more senior position on the campaign than Mr. Page, the two men had a myriad of contacts in Russia. They would indeed go on to leverage these contacts throughout the campaign to put themselves in a better situation financially and professionally.

Mr. Manafort and Mr. Page were also featured prominently in the Trump dossier, put together by ex-British intelligence officer Christopher Steele. Mr. Steele wrote throughout the summer of 2016 that Mr. Manafort and Mr. Page acted as key liaisons between the Trump team and the Russian government. Though some of the dossier remains uncorroborated, many details have been confirmed as the investigation into the Trump campaign's contacts with Russia trudges forward.

"Speaking in confidence to a compatriot in late July 2016, Source B, an ethnic Russian close associate of Republican US presidential candidate Donald TRUMP, admitted that there was a well-developed conspiracy of cooperation between them and the Russian leadership," wrote Mr. Steele.

"This is managed on the TRUMP side by the Republican candidate's campaign manager, Paul MANAFORT, who was using foreign policy advisor, Carter PAGE, and others as intermediaries. The two sides had a mutual interest in defeating Democratic presidential candidate Hillary CLINTON, whom President PUTIN apparently both hated and feared."

Mr. Page's alleged activities during the 2016 campaign prompted the FBI to seek a request to surveil Mr. Page's communications under the Foreign Intelligence Surveillance Act (FISA). In October 2016, after

Mr. Page had left the Trump campaign, the first of four FISA requests on Mr. Page was issued. The government argued that Mr. Page was acting as an undeclared foreign agent of Russia. The FISA on Mr. Page has become the backbone of many conspiracy theories spread by some Republicans looking to discredit the Mueller probe. Instead of refuting the serious allegations written by Mr. Steele and the Department of Justice, Representative Devin Nunes and others have relied on attacking the process by which the information was gathered.

One of the most damning reports written by Mr. Steele alleged that Mr. Page, during his documented July 2016 trip to Moscow, secretly met with Igor Sechin, a former KGB agent-turned-public official considered one of the few men in Vladimir Putin's inner circle. Numerous press reports have declared Mr. Sechin as the second-most-powerful man in Russia, only behind Mr. Putin. Mr. Sechin is the CEO of the Russian state oil company Rosneft, after assuming full control over the multi-billion dollar company in 2012.

"Speaking in July 2016, a Russian source close to Rosneft President, PUTIN close associate and US-sanctioned individual, Igor SECHIN, confided the details of a recent secret meeting between him and visiting Foreign Affairs Advisor to Republican presidential candidate Donald TRUMP, Carter PAGE," Steele wrote on July 25th.

"According to SECHIN's associate, the Rosneft President (CEO) had raised with PAGE the issues of future bilateral energy cooperation and prospects for an associated move to lift Ukraine-related western sanctions against Russia."

At the time of Mr. Page's July trip to Russia, Rosneft was seeking to sell a chunk of its shares in what would become one of Russia's biggest privatization deals in decades. The company ended up selling 19.5% (worth approximately $11 billion) of its shares to the Swiss multinational commodity trader Glencore and the Qatar Investment Authority, though the purchase was conducted using a series of shell companies, making it impossible to determine the true ownership. The sale was announced in December 2016 as Mr. Page made a second trip to Russia.

Approximately three months after his first memo on the secret meeting between Mr. Page and Mr. Sechin, Mr. Steele added more details from information he learned from his sources: "In terms of the substance of their discussion, SECHIN's associate said that the Rosneft President was so keen to lift personal and corporate western sanctions imposed on the company, that he offered PAGE associates the brokerage of up to a 19 per cent (privatised) stake in Rosneft in return PAGE had expressed interest."

A brokerage fee of the sale would have been worth tens or even hundreds of millions of dollars. In multiple FISA renewals on Mr. Page, the Department of Justice, according to House Democrats, subsequently "provided additional information obtained through multiple independent sources that corroborated Steele's reporting." Though the specific claim about Mr. Page and members of the Trump campaign being offered a portion of the Rosneft sale has never been confirmed, US investigators appear to have multiple other sources that support Steele's intelligence.

Sometime after Mr. Page left the Trump campaign in 2016, a little-known energy company based in Las Vegas with partners in the Middle East made a startling claim on their website: Carter Page's Global Energy Capital made a $350 million capital commitment to the small investment company. Where did Mr. Page's small company come up with more than a third of a billion dollars? My investigation into the alleged capital commitment revealed a highly misleading Congressional testimony from Mr. Page and a desperate effort on the part of the Las Vegas company to cover their tracks and distance themselves from the former Trump adviser.

The Process

My investigation into Mr. Page and his alleged dealings with RD Heritage Group relied heavily on human sources. Unfortunately, due to this fact, I cannot share much about my process in uncovering this information.

Responding to a tip from a couple Twitter followers, I followed the trail of Carter Page's business ventures and ended up with RD Heritage Group. Apart from the eye-popping amount of money allegedly pledged by Mr. Page, I was shocked at the incredible responsiveness of those involved with RD Heritage.

Unfortunately, they were responsive to my queries for all the wrong reasons, immediately scrubbing their website of any mentions of Mr. Page.

Their efforts to re-write history were unsuccessful, though, as I came prepared with receipts.

————

August 11, 2018
Energy Investment Group Claims $350M Capital Commitment from Carter Page

The group made the claim after Page advised Trump

An investment company based in Las Vegas, with oil and gas interests in the Middle East, claimed that they received a commitment of more than three hundred million dollars from Carter Page's Global Energy Capital after Page's involvement in the Trump campaign.

The investment company, RD Heritage Group, claimed on their website that they secured a capital commitment of hundreds of millions of dollars from Page and his company:

> "$350MM capital commitment by Global Energy Capital . . . an investment management and advisory firm focused on the energy sector primarily in emerging markets. Global Energy Capital was founded by Carter Page, CFA. Carter has spent 7 years as an investment banker at Merrill Lynch in London, Moscow and New York . . . Carter was also a foreign policy advisor to Presidential candidate Donald Trump."

It is unclear if Page ever actually followed through with his commitment. The exact timing of the alleged partnership between RD Heritage and Global Energy Capital is unknown, though it happened after Carter Page's involvement with the Trump campaign.

In his November 2017 testimony to Congress, Page testified under oath that he had "no other income beyond [passive] investments" in 2016 and

2017. When asked to clarify his statements by Representative Swalwell, Page reiterated that he no clients in 2016 and 2017 and he had no income.

> MR. SWALWELL: Well, I guess I want to understand, Mr. Page, if you haven't had any clients in 2017 and 2016 and your only source of income were investments, it seems to me that you would be pretty aware of where your income was coming from in 2016.   And you're telling us that you can't recall.
>
> MR. PAGE: I'm saying there was no other income beyond investments, yeah.

> MR. SWALWELL: What has your source of income been in 2017, if any?
>
> MR. PAGE: There are no sources of income right now.   I'm living off savings. I'm burning through savings.
>
> MR. SWALWELL: What were your sources of income in 2016?
>
> MR. PAGE: Investments that I have, passive investments.

With no clients, no income, and no public business transactions, it is entirely unclear how Page's company could commit $350M to RD Heritage. Emails, messages, and calls to RD Heritage, its manager John Dean Harper, founder Robert Davis, and Page over the course of weeks were not answered or returned.

The registered address of RD Heritage is a mailbox located within a UPS store in Las Vegas. The only other publicly announced business deal that RD Heritage has struck since its inception in 2013 was earlier this year with LeanLife Health, a Canadian pharmaceutical company. RD Heritage and all of its partners are not accused of any wrongdoing.

———

Less than forty-eight hours after the first emails and messages were sent to RD Heritage requesting comment, the company scrubbed their website of any mention of Page or Global Energy Capital. The paragraph detailing Page's investment was subsequently altered to read, "$350MM capital commitment from an energy focused fund."

A cached version of the website saved the original description of Page's involvement; as of July 24, 2018, the RD Heritage website text read:

Energy Investments
$350MM capital commitment by Global Energy Capital . . . Global Energy Capital is an investment management and advisory firm focused on the energy sector primarily in emerging markets. Global Energy Capital was founded by Carter Page, CFA. Carter has spent 7 years as an investment banker at Merrill Lynch in London, Moscow and New York where he most recently served as Chief Operating Officer of the Energy and Power Group. He was involved in over $25 billion of transactions in the energy and power sector. He spent 3 years in Moscow where he was responsible for the opening of the Merrill office and was an advisor on key transactions for Gazprom, RAO UES and others. Previously, Carter was a Fellow at the Council on Foreign Relations where he was responsible for energy-related research on the Caspian Sea region. He is a graduate of the United States Naval Academy, holds a MBA from the Stern School of Business at New York University and is a Chartered Financial Analyst. Carter was also a foreign policy advisor to Presidential candidate Donald Trump

And as of July 25, 2018, one day after being contacted and asked for comment, the RD Heritage website text was changed to read:

Energy Investments
$350MM capital commitment from an energy focused fund, with energy sector primarily in emerging markets. Then later, RD Heritage partnered with the MHA Nation (Mandan, Hidatsa and Arikara tribes) who committed up to $100MM along with a $2B private equity firm in a management buyout of a public company's E&P assets in N. Dakota

———

RD Heritage's main partner in the Middle East is Hadi Al Alawi of the Al

Hayat Group, a Bahrain investment company. The company's website features pictures of one of its principals, Robert Davis, alongside Alawi and various Gulf government officials. The group also touts relationships with major oil/gas companies such as Qatar Petroleum, Kuwait Petroleum, and Saudi Aramco.

A *Bloomberg* profile of Page in 2016 featured a photo of the then-Trump adviser with Mr. Alawi, confirming that there exists a relationship between the two.

The question of how and why Page was in a position to commit $350,000,000 to a relatively obscure investment company remains completely unknown. Multiple banking experts with whom I spoke cast doubt on the possibility that this money could've been a loan from a bank. Page, being the subject of a publicly reported FISA warrant that claimed he was a secret agent of Russia, would've been a risky client for any bank.

Page testified that he had no income in 2016 and 2017 except for "passive investments" in publicly traded companies, and that he was "burning through savings." If he truly did commit $350M in capital to RD Heritage Group after his tenure as a Trump adviser, his Congressional testimony appears to have been misleading or incomplete at best.

Cambridge Analytica

Who's Who:
- **Cambridge Analytica:** Data analysis company hired by Mr. Cruz, Mr. Carson, and then Mr. Trump.
- **Julian Wheatland:** Cambridge Analytica executive.
- **Samuel Patten:** Republican political consultant and lobbyist who contracted with Cambridge Analytica.

An area of continuing interest to Mr. Mueller and his team of investigators has been the role that data analysis and political consulting firm Cambridge Analytica played during the 2016 election. Founded and funded by former Trump campaign chief executive Steve Bannon and

Republican mega-donors Robert and Rebekah Mercer, Cambridge Analytica was established in 2013 as a branch of the British SCL Group, a behavioral research and strategic communication company.

Cambridge Analytica first became involved in the US in 2014, when they forayed into the midterm elections, supporting over three-dozen candidates in various races. Most candidates hired Cambridge Analytica because of its ability to identify voters who were responsive to a specific message and then target these voters with ads that supported the candidate's position on the topic about which they had concerns. This practice became known as micro-targeting because of its extreme precision in persuading very specific clusters of voters to support a candidate.

In order to successfully complete the micro-targeting, Cambridge Analytica broke a litany of rules in secretly harvesting the personal data of over fifty million Facebook users. This gave the company secret insights into the tendencies, interests, and locations of voters.

This strategy of micro-targeting made Cambridge Analytica very attractive to Republican candidates in the 2016 primary elections. The firm was first hired by Ted Cruz to the tune of $3 million in the weeks leading up to the first primary elections in Iowa. The Cruz campaign continued to use Cambridge Analytica's services and ended up paying the company a total of $5.8 million.

Ben Carson then hired Cambridge Analytica for a brief period of work before the Mercers decided that they needed to support the clear front-runner for the Republican nomination, Donald Trump.

Mr. Mueller's interest in Cambridge Analytica's work appears to be focused on three main areas of concern that could possibly connect the firm to Russian interference: First, investigating the data operation and micro-targeting of voters and whether any of this information was shared with Russians who were targeting Americans for the purposes of swaying the election to Mr. Trump. Second, tracing Cambridge Analytica's outreach to WikiLeaks in an attempt to weaponize the emails stolen by Russian intelligence. Finally, as Mr. Mueller usually does in nearly every facet of his investigation, following the money trail with Cambridge Analytica to determine if any financial transactions were improperly or illegally consummated.

The Cambridge Analytica data operation in support of the Trump campaign is a complex web of highly technical efforts to get inside the minds of the American electorate. According to their website in early 2016, the firm said, "We collect up to 5,000 data points on over 220 million Americans . . . to model target audience groups and predict the behavior of like-minded people."

After whistleblower Chris Wylie exposed the scandal of Cambridge Analytica stealing and harvesting the Facebook data, the company's data ties to Russia quickly began to become unearthed. Wylie explained in detail how Cambridge Analytica offered multiple presentations touting its services to the Russian oil company Lukoil, including its ability to spread disinformation and sway voters. Wylie found this outreach especially strange given that an oil company in Russia should have no interest in any political election operations.

"I kept asking Alexander, 'Can you explain to me what they want?'" Wylie said. "I don't understand why Lukoil wants to know about political targeting in America."

Though not officially a government entity, Lukoil receives support from the Russian government and its CEO meets with Mr. Putin regularly. During testimony to the US Senate in March 2018, Mr. Wylie also disclosed that Cambridge Analytica "used Russian researchers to gather its data" in parallel to the Facebook data harvesting.

Their outreach to WikiLeaks came in the summer of 2016 from Alexander Nix, then-CEO of Cambridge Analytica. Mr. Nix, according to media reports, emailed the leader of WikiLeaks, Julian Assange, and asked for the 33,000 deleted emails off of Mrs. Clinton's private email server. Contrary to popular belief at the time, there is no evidence that Mr. Assange ever had these emails, as none of them have ever been made public.

The emails that Mr. Assange and WikiLeaks did possess were stolen by Russian intelligence services from the Democratic National Committee (DNC) and John Podesta, a top Clinton aide. Mr. Nix asked for these emails as well, in an effort to index and weaponize the content of the emails for the campaign or a pro-Trump political action committee to use. Mr. Nix forwarded his outreach to WikiLeaks to the Mercers and others in the Trump orbit. Mr. Assange has publicly stated, "I can confirm an approach by Cambridge Analytica [prior to November last year] and can confirm that it was rejected by WikiLeaks."

It's important to note that as far as the public is concerned, the entire narrative around this exchange has been shaped by Mr. Nix and Mr. Assange, two men not known for their honesty. BBC correspondent Paul Wood reported in mid-2018 that a Cambridge Analytica employee told a lawyer that the company "had the Clinton emails more than a month before they were published by WikiLeaks." This report has not been corroborated as of yet, but Mr. Mueller continues to investigate. He has requested scores of documents from Cambridge Analytica, including emails from the executives, and has conducted interviews with the data team on the Trump campaign. The role that Mr. Bannon played in Cambridge Analytica's work for the Trump election effort is also under scrutiny by various investigators in Washington, DC.

Finally, the money trail of Cambridge Analytica, SCL Group, and at least some of their employees has garnered the attention of investigators in the U.K. and the United States. In late August 2018, Mr. Mueller charged a Cambridge Analytica contractor, Samuel Patten, with one count of working as an unregistered agent for a Ukrainian oligarch and his political party, Opposition Bloc, which also employed Mr. Manafort. Mr. Patten pleaded guilty to funneling at least $50,000 from the Ukrainian oligarch into Mr. Trump's inauguration committee. It is illegal for foreigners to make such a donation.

Mr. Patten's guilty plea also included details about his lobbying work for the Ukrainian oligarch and his pro-Russia opposition party. In support of his lobbying efforts, Mr. Patten hired a name that keeps appearing in the Trump-Russia scandal: Konstantin Kilimnik.

Mr. Kilimnik, if you'll recall, has strong connections to Russian intelligence and acted as a conduit between Mr. Manafort and Mr. Deripaska during the campaign. Around the same time, Mr. Kilimnik was working with Mr. Patten in his representation of the Ukrainian political party.

Mr. Kilimnik and Mr. Patten were paid over $1 million for their consulting work for the Ukrainians. According to Mr. Wylie, the Cambridge Analytica whistleblower, Mr. Patten contracted with the firm and did work in Africa as well as the United States.

Mr. Patten "was responsible for CA operations in the US that involved covertly testing US voter attitudes on Putin's leadership," Mr. Wylie announced in a Tweet following Mr. Patten's guilty plea. He added, "I know there's more to come . . ."

I actually had contact with Mr. Patten in March of 2018, well before his guilty plea. I was among the first to discover his partnership with Mr. Kilimnik and their company, which ended up being cited in Mr. Mueller's statement of criminal information. I exchanged a few emails with Mr. Patten, but he insisted that there was nothing untoward about his work with Mr. Kilimnik. He ended our email exchange with, "I've been responding to various media requests on this general subject for going on two years, and it's getting real old. There's not a story here, and I am not interested in being quoted."

Wanting to learn more about the money behind some of the principals of Cambridge Analytica and SCL Group, I began to dig into their various business interests. Who better to start with than the man who controlled the money for SCL Group, their CFO, Julian Wheatland?

The Process

Running a quick search on my favorite open-source business registry for Julian Wheatland returned thirty-five results, with the vast majority of the businesses with which Mr. Wheatland was involved focusing on data and finance, as his background would suggest. One company stood out from the other thirty-four because it was not in Mr. Wheatland's area of study or his professional resume. The oil and gas energy company, Phi Energy Limited, had a short lifespan of just over two years, with Mr. Wheatland being involved for less than that.

I pulled the company documents for Phi Energy Limited for free from the UK government (on the day of my college graduation!) and was immediately struck by the odd shareholder structure. As previously discussed at length, almost half of the business conducted in Cyprus is at the behest of Russian individuals. Why, then, was a Cyprus shell company part-owner of a European oil and gas venture?

The details didn't add up. After conducting an interview with one of the other people involved in Phi Energy Limited, during which the man lied numerous times, I knew something was amiss.

What I found was not surprising, but still newsworthy, nevertheless: Russian fingerprints.

———————

July 17, 2018
Company Part-Owned by Chairman of SCL Group Sought €200 Million Investment from Russians in 2015

As Cambridge Analytica was pitching to prospective political clients in the United States, including Ted Cruz and Donald Trump, the Chairman of their parent company was seeking €200 million from Russian-speaking investors for his new oil and gas venture.

In late 2014, SCL Group Chairman and future CEO of Cambridge Analytica Julian Wheatland became a Director in a London oil and gas company called Phi Energy Limited.

As of November 2015, Wheatland had no ownership interest in Phi Energy. In December 2015, that changed, and Wheatland acquired 3,500 shares in the company. Also involved were Tarick Kreimeia (via his company Navitas Holdings), a Wheatland business partner in a finance and project development company, and Ennio Senese, a Dutch corporate executive.

Sometime in 2015, the group hired Stanislav Novak, a Russian translator based in Ukraine. Novak was tasked with translating an investment teaser from English to Russian. The teaser explained that Phi Energy was looking for a €200 million investment in order to purchase a refinery in Northern Europe.

After being asked for comment in early July, Novak's resume, which mentioned his work for Phi Energy, was deleted from the website of his translating company. A cyber-security expert explained that the deletion appeared to be a specific action and not the result of a mistake: "The upload area is still accessible from the web. So they both removed that file, and updated the robots.txt to explicitly make all the search engines dump the caches."

Company Name: **PHI ENERGY LIMITED**

X43CQMY1

Company Number: **09150937**

Received for filing in Electronic Format on the: **17/03/2015**

New *Appointment* Details

Date of Appointment: 24/12/2014

Name: MR JULIAN DAVID WHEATLAND

Consented to Act: **YES**

Service Address recorded as Company's registered office

Full Details of Shareholders

The details below relate to individuals / corporate bodies that were shareholders as at 27/11/2015 or that had ceased to be shareholders since the made up date of the previous Annual Return

A full list of shareholders for the company are shown below

Shareholding 1 : **15000 ORDINARY shares held as at the date of this return**
Name: **NAVITAS HOLDINGS LIMITED**

Shareholding 2 : **15000 ORDINARY shares held as at the date of this return**
Name: **ENNIO SENESE**

Shareholding 3 : **15000 ORDINARY shares held as at the date of this return**
Name: **RAVICA HOLDINGS LIMITED**

Full Details of Shareholders

The details below relate to individuals / corporate bodies that were shareholders as at 31/12/2015 or that had ceased to be shareholders since the made up date of the previous Annual Return

A full list of shareholders for the company are shown below

Shareholding 1 : **15500 ORDINARY shares held as at the date of this return**
Name: **NAVITAS HOLDINGS LIMITED**

Shareholding 2 : **15500 ORDINARY shares held as at the date of this return**
Name: **ENNIO SENESE**

Shareholding 3 : **15500 ORDINARY shares held as at the date of this return**
Name: **RAVICA HOLDINGS LIMITED**

Shareholding 4 : **3500 ORDINARY shares held as at the date of this return**
Name: **JULIAN WHEATLAND**

In an email, Novak confirmed his work for Phi Energy but declined to comment further, citing the existence of a Non-Disclosure Agreement.

It is unclear if any Russians ended up investing in the project. Phi Energy was dissolved in late 2016.

Mysterious LLC

The fourth shareholder, and as of late 2015, a business partner with the SCL Group Chairman, was a Cypriot shell company (Ravica Holdings) with links to powerful Russians. The sole Director of the company which held shares in Phi Energy along with Wheatland was a Cypriot woman named Sofia Iosif.

Iosif, via a Russian conglomerate called Interros, manages billions of dollars' worth of assets for the Russian oligarch Vladimir Potanin. Since at least 2006, Potanin has entrusted Iosif with nominally owning Interros, a company in which billions of dollars flows annually. Iosif was named in divorce proceedings between Potanin and his estranged wife. 2014 audited accounts for Interros show that the shareholders took home over $861,000,000 in dividend income. With her 45% stake, Iosif would've handled at least $387,000,000 of Potanin's money in 2014 alone—the year when Wheatland joined Phi Energy as a Director.

The ultimate owner of Ravica Holdings, one of the three other shareholders in Phi Energy alongside Wheatland, is Cyproservus Co. Limited, an affiliate of the Cypriot law-firm of Chrysses Demetriades. Cyproservus provides services to at least 2,600 active companies, making it impossible to determine the true ownership of Ravica Holdings.

Interros, the Potanin/Russian conglomerate that was the controlling shareholder of the world's largest producer of palladium, Norilsk Nickel, also uses Cyproservus. Because of this, the two share the same registered office space in a building in Nicosia, Cyprus, along with at least 1,000 other registered companies.

A partner of the law firm affiliated with Cyproservus, Pavlina Constantinides, made the following statement:

> "Due to professional ethics I am not in a position to provide to any third party any information on Ravica Holdings Limited (the "Company") unless I receive our clients' authorisation in this respect."

2009.02.03 - 2009.02.04 ↓ [Inactive]

VLADIMIR POTANIN

Address: Skatertniy Pereulok, 7-3, Moscow, Russia
Country of Citizenship: **Russia**

50.000 Shares [2,50%]
Class: **ORDINARY**, Currency: **USD**, Unit Value: 1

ΣΟΦΙΑ ΙΩΣΗΦ (SOFIA JOSEPH)

Address: Hippocrates, 6, Saint John, 3016, Limassol, Cyprus
Country of Citizenship: **Cyprus**

500 Shares [0,02%]
Class: **ORDINARY**, Currency: **EUR**, Unit Value: 1

975.000 Shares [48,73%]
Class: **ORDINARY**, Currency: **USD**, Unit Value: 1

INTERROS INTERNATIONAL INVESTMENTS LIMITED

2006.10.19 — 2008.01.21
MEGASHARE INVESTMENTS LIMITED

Reg. Number	Type	SubType
HE 185865	**Limited Company**	**Private**

Registration Date	Organisation Status	Objects
19/10/2006	**Active**	**Investment operations and other**

Addresses   Directors & Secretaries   Shareholders   Documents (55)

👥 SHAREHOLDERS

2014.11.25 ↓ [Active]

TACOM HOLDING S.A.

Address: **ESTATE PAST, Road Town, Tortola, British Virgin Islands**

220.000 Shares [9,91%]
Class: **ORDINARY**, Currency: **USD**, Unit Value: 0,01

ΣΟΦΙΑ ΙΩΣΗΦ (SOFIA JOSEPH)

Address: Hippocrates, 6, Saint John, 3016, Limassol, Cyprus
Country of Citizenship: **Cyprus**

500 Shares [0,02%]
Class: **ORDINARY**, Currency: **EUR**, Unit Value: 1

1.000.000 Shares [45,02%]
Class: **ORDINARY**, Currency: **USD**, Unit Value: 1

INTERROS INTERNATIONAL INVESTMENTS LIMITED

NOTES TO THE FINANCIAL STATEMENTS
Year ended 31 December 2014

4. Critical accounting estimates and judgements (continued)

•   **Impairment of investments in subsidiaries/associates**

The Company periodically evaluates the recoverability of investments in subsidiaries/associates whenever indicators of impairment are present. Indicators of impairment include such items as declines in revenues, earnings or cash flows or material adverse changes in the economic or political stability of a particular country, which may indicate that the carrying amount of an asset is not recoverable. If facts and circumstances indicate that investment in subsidiaries/associates may be impaired, the estimated future discounted cash flows associated with these subsidiaries/associates would be compared to their carrying amounts to determine if a write-down to fair value is necessary.

5. Operating income

	2014	2013
	USD	USD
Dividend income	861,356,884	194,752,156
	861,356,884	194,752,156

RAVICA HOLDINGS LIMITED

2009.07.16 — 2015.01.13
GASTONIO TRADING LIMITED

Reg. Number	Type	SubType
HE 252502	Limited Company	Private

Registration Date	Organisation Status	Objects
16/07/2009	Active	General trade and other

Addresses   Directors & Secretaries   Shareholders   Documents (13)

📖 ADDRESSES

Arch. Makarios III, 284, FORTUNA COURT, BLOCK B, Floor 2, 3105, Limassol, Cyprus Active from 2009.07.16

INTERROS INTERNATIONAL INVESTMENTS LIMITED

2006.10.19 — 2008.01.21
MEGASHARE INVESTMENTS LIMITED

Reg. Number	Type	SubType
HE 185865	Limited Company	Private

Registration Date	Organisation Status	Objects
19/10/2006	Active	Investment operations and other

Addresses   Directors & Secretaries   Shareholders   Documents (55)

📖 ADDRESSES

Arch. Makarios III, 284, FORTUNA COURT BLOCK B, Floor 2, 3105, Limassol, Cyprus Active from 2006.10.19

Registered office address for both Ravica Holdings and Interros, located in Nicosia, Cyprus.

As of this writing, Ravica Holdings hasn't authorized any disclosures. When asked for more specific information on the type of services Cyproservus provides and for how many companies it acts as a shareholder, Constantinides said, "We are unable to assist you any further in this matter."

Interview with Phi Energy CEO

The CEO and additional shareholder of Phi Energy, Ennio Senese, exchanged messages with this reporter over the course of a couple weeks. Many of his comments were provably false based on corporate documents filed with the UK Companies House, and other open-source information. Senese denied any Russian involvement in the company.

When asked for information about Ravica Holdings, Senese said, "Ravica wasn't a shareholder of Phi when I was there." In truth, however, Ravica and Senese were two of the three shareholders in Phi Energy as of February 2015, and that remained true until the day the company was dissolved.

Full Details of Shareholders

The details below relate to individuals / corporate bodies that were shareholders as at 19/02/2015 or that had ceased to be shareholders since the made up date of the previous Annual Return

A full list of shareholders for the company are shown below

Shareholding 1	: **15000 ORDINARY shares held as at the date of this return**
Name:	**TARICK KREIMEIA**
Shareholding 2	: **15000 ORDINARY shares held as at the date of this return**
Name:	**ENNIO SENESE**
Shareholding 3	: **15000 ORDINARY shares held as at the date of this return**
Name:	**RAVICA HOLDINGS LIMITED**

When given another opportunity to explain his relationship with Ravica Holdings days after the first messages were exchanged, Senese stuck to his original proclamation, "I was the CEO of Phi and Ravica was not in play . . . I was the CEO from inception until Jan 2016 more or less. Ravica was never involved."

After the Russian translator confirmed his work for Phi Energy, this reporter reached out to Senese again and asked, "Why did Phi hire a Russian translator?" This time, Senese was more blunt with his response: "We didn't."

When shown proof that Ravica Holdings was indeed involved when he was CEO and shareholder, Senese said he had "No clue . . . Also, quite frankly, I don't care about it either." Senese gave the name of a Danish businessman who he said was behind a Cyprus LLC that was involved in Phi Energy, though he didn't believe this was the same entity as Ravica Holdings.

Senese was then shown the work of the Russian translator, whom he denied hiring. The ex-CEO of Phi Energy said, "I don't remember this," though he later confirmed that he wrote the English half of the translated investment teaser.

Phi Energy was also registered in the Netherlands, where Senese resides. To avoid any possible confusion about the role of Ravica Holdings, company documents for the Dutch company were reviewed, confirming that the UK company was the parent group.

A 21-page brochure published in 2014 outlining Phi Energy's business and key people lists Wheatland as the Chief Financial Officer. The brochure read:

JULIAN WHEATLAND / Chief Financial Officer

Mr. Wheatland is an experienced financier and international project development expert.

Prior to Phi Energy he was the founder and also CEO of Hatton International, which is a finance and project development company specialising in cross-border and inward investment transactions, with a focus on international trade and economic development in emerging economies. Hatton International has access to a wide base of commercial and government relationships and it manages and delivers projects from conception to realisation. Hatton works with international defence and aerospace companies to help them fulfil their economic development and investment commitments to customer countries (offsets); it has successfully implemented projects in North America, South Africa, the Middle East and Eastern Europe.

Before founding Hatton, Mr. Wheatland was head of the International Investment Division at the UK structured finance house, Consensus Business Group. At Consensus he built an $800m international investment portfolio and developed FDI projects in international markets.

Prior to Consensus, Julian was a Founder of Edengene, the specialist strategic innovation business and was a Managing Consultant at PA Consulting, where he was an authority on entrepreneurial venture development.

Julian read electrical and electronic engineering at The University of Leeds and has an MBA from The Wharton School. He is a Chartered Engineer and is Non-Executive Chairman of Strategic Communication Laboratories, the leading international communications and behavioural influence company.

Its alleged partners included oil and gas companies in the United States, Europe, the Middle East, and Asia, including Shell, Noble Group, Eni, Esso,

BP, Statoil, Tamoil, Total, Saras, Energy Institute, Statoil Fuel & Retail, and Tüpraş.

In 2015, Phi Energy declared itself a dormant company to the UK Companies House, allowing it to avoid filing any financial information.

Wheatland did not respond to multiple requests for comment. It remains unclear if any Russian investors ultimately participated in Phi Energy.

A Confession in Plain Sight

Who's Who:

- **Konstantin Rykov:** Russian government internet pioneer, propagandist, and former politician.
- **Yulia Alferova:** Employee of Aras Agalarov's business empire who helped organize Miss Universe 2013.

One of the more staggering aspects of the Trump–Russia story came via a notorious Russian propagandist with connections to politics, television, brothels, internet trolls, and everything in between. To date, mainstream media has only reported on the topic in passing, leaving those who have read the full story of Konstantin Rykov frustrated and despondent.

Mr. Rykov first rose to prominence in Russia during the internet boom of the late 1990s and early 2000s. As a young twenty-something, he created websites and drove online conversation on a multitude of topics ranging from pornography to talent shows to politics.

"Starting in the 1990s, Rykov built a kingdom of popular websites beginning with fuck.ru, an obscenity-laced website that flaunted Russia's rules while he operated under the pseudonym Jason Foris," noted Patrick Howell O'Neill, a cybersecurity reporter. "He expanded into website design, advertising networks, book publishing, television, and eventually hundreds of other internet projects, according to his own count."

Mr. Rykov's tech-savvy skills soon caught the attention of those in charge in Russia, who understood that the power of the internet was going to play a major role in politics moving forward. He landed a job at Russia's state-owned Channel One as the head of the internet department in 2002, officially becoming an employee of the Russian government. The notoriety from Channel One prompted Mr. Rykov to create his own newspaper called *Vzglyad* (vizz-glee-adh).

The reputation of *Vzglyad* among Western observers quickly turned negative as it became a mouthpiece for Mr. Putin's Kremlin, kept under the close watch of Mr. Putin's deputy chief of staff and one of his closest aides, Vladislav Surkov. Critics of the Putin government have alleged that Mr. Surkov even arranged for private funding of Mr. Rykov's activities. In any event, *Vzglyad* morphed into a propaganda machine for Mr. Putin's government, churning out positive stories about the regime and spreading disinformation about its enemies.

"There were weekly meetings at the presidential administration," said the editor-in-chief of *Vzglyad* in 2007 and 2008. "Sometimes, there were situations when we published something, and Surkov's assistant who was in charge of the media . . . called and said, 'No, please, replace this article,' or, 'Please, publish something about this issue.'"

While heading *Vzglyad*, Mr. Rykov branched out and founded what would become Russia's largest brothel, run entirely online. The website, called Dosug, has been likened to something like Uber for sex, and has sex workers all across Europe on a social media-like platform. Dosug's popularity on the strange world of the dark web has turned into a money-maker for Mr. Rykov. He purchased a $2 million villa in France and bragged to Russian media about his net worth.

His success online with political newspapers such as *Vzglyad* and "social" websites that attracted the attention of many Russian men made Mr. Rykov a force to be reckoned with. He ran for the State Duma (the equivalent of the House of Representatives in the United States) in Mr. Putin's United Russia party and was elected in 2007 to represent the city of Nizhny, with a population of over one million people.

At the end of his term in 2011, Mr. Rykov had nearly a decade of mutual support from the Kremlin and those close to Vladimir Putin. He stepped away from his position in the Russian government and became a "private" citizen, still wielding an incredible amount of political power. In 2013, one of Mr. Rykov's close friends, Artem Klyushin, an internet troll who was previously arrested for scamming a casino and winning large sums of money by bribing a dealer, was pictured with Mr. Trump during the Miss Universe pageant in Moscow.

Mr. Klyushin's then-wife, Yulia, worked as an event organizer for the Agalarov family who hosted Miss Universe, and was particularly involved in the planning of the 2013 pageant. She was particularly close to Emin Agalarov, according to a source, and often interacted with him on social media. Alferova posted multiple pictures of Mr. Trump in Moscow and sat in on at least one of his meetings with Russian officials.

The infamous Steele dossier alleged that the Russian government had blackmail on Mr. Trump from video showing him with prostitutes during his 2013 trip. It was Emin Agalarov, according to reports, who offered to send prostitutes to Mr. Trump's hotel room in Moscow, though all men involved deny that this ended up happening. Mr. Agalarov, though, through his association with the Klyushins and thus Mr. Rykov and Dosug, would've certainly had the opportunity to do so.

By 2014, Mr. Rykov was directly involved with dirty Kremlin tricks, allegedly liasing between French presidential candidate Marine Le Pen and the Russian government. After the purchase of the upscale villa in France in the 2000s, Mr. Rykov apparently established contacts within French political circles and was able to act as a go-between for Le Pen and Kremlin officials.

In 2015, his attention turned to the Trump campaign. He created a Russian language, pro-Trump website with a Russian domain, Trump2016.ru, and was not shy about his support for Mr. Trump to his hundreds of thousands of followers on Twitter and other social media sites.

On election night, Mr. Rykov attended a party with Mr. Klyushin and celebrated as they watched Mr. Trump's victory. It was what Mr. Rykov posted on social media after the election, though, that caught my attention and the attention of other researchers into possible coordination between the Trump campaign and the Russian government.

In an extraordinary confession of sorts, Mr. Rykov posted a two-part series on Facebook alleging that he worked with hacker groups, WikiLeaks, and Cambridge Analytica to swing the election in Mr. Trump's favor.

Although his involvement remains uncorroborated, the details that Mr. Rykov included in his posts eventually were substantiated.

He was correct that WikiLeaks was the vehicle that the Russian government used to disseminate the hacked emails stolen from the Clinton campaign and the Democrats, as the US intelligence community would conclude two months after Mr. Rykov's posts. He was correct about Cambridge Analytica's role in creating detailed voter prototypes, as various media reports would confirm more than a year after his posts.

The confession on Facebook and subsequent research into Mr. Rykov's proximity to Vladimir Putin resulted in two of my investigatory articles.

The Process

Responding to a tip from a Reddit user, I found the following Facebook posts from Mr. Rykov and was stunned that they hadn't been covered by any media organizations. I did a detailed background on Mr. Rykov via open-source searching and found his connections to Marine Le Pen and related political scandals in France. I limited my Google results to only include only websites from France or in French, and was able to uncover the information about Mr. Rykov's French real estate.

Having already done a fair amount of research on Mr. Klyushin and his wife Yulia Alferova, I was surprised to see them come up during a cursory search of Mr. Rykov's tweets. To learn more about this relationship, I used the Twitter Advanced Search function and filtered Mr. Rykov's Tweets to include only those where he tagged Mr. Klyushin or Ms. Alferova. The search returned dozens of results, confirming to me that the relationship between the three was indeed very close.

I then made sure to search Mr. Rykov's full name in Russian (Константин Рыков) on the Russian search engine Yandex, which often includes some results that you wouldn't find on Google or another United States-based search engine. Sifting through pages of image results on Yandex paid off, as I came across a blog that included an image of an official-looking badge with Mr. Rykov's name. I contacted my Russian-speaking friend, Lorenz Cohen, and he translated the document, which indicated that Mr. Rykov was a "trusted confidant" of Mr. Putin's during the 2012 election.

Confirming the authenticity of the image from the blog proved to be difficult but necessary. Getting in touch with a few of my Russian media-savvy journalist connections, who are much smarter than myself in the world of Russian politics, led me to uncover more about these "trusted confidants" and their role. I was informed that these people have to be officially listed and declared by the candidate running, in this case Mr. Putin. Navigating to Mr. Putin's 2012 electoral website, I was able to find the list of declared "trusted confidants" and spotted the name I was looking for—Константин Рыков—Konstantin Rykov.

This information on Mr. Rykov formed the premise of my two investigatory articles into the seemingly omnipresent Kremlin propagandist.

November 21, 2017
Kremlin Propagandist Boasted of His Hacking Efforts, Strongly Implied Colluding with Trump Team in Facebook Posts

A former Duma deputy with close ties to Putin made the posts less than a week after Donald Trump won the election.

On November 12th, 2016, just days after Donald Trump was elected President, a Russian man named Konstantin Rykov posted on Facebook detailing how "Donald and I decided to free America and make it great again." In a two-part series that reads like a fantasy novel, Rykov illustrated in detail the four-year effort to elect Trump.

Excerpts of the Facebook posts are below. Translations by Lorenz Cohen:

Part One

It's time for wonderful stories. I'll tell you about (now it's possible) how Donald Trump and I decided to free America and make it great again. This took us as much as 4 years and 2 more days.

It all started at night from 6 to 7 November 2012.

[Trump] lifted his plane to the sky and flew between New York and DC, calling the whole world through his twitter—to start a march on Washington!

Without a moment's thought, I wrote him a replay, which sounded like this in Russian: "I'm ready." What should I do?

Suddenly! There was a thin squeak of warning in the DM.

It was a message from Donald Trump. More precisely a picture. In the picture he was sitting in the armchair of his jet, smiling cheerfully and showing me the thumb of his right hand.

Part Two

What was our idea with Donald Trump?

For four years and two days .. it was necessary to get to everyone in the brain and grab all possible means of mass perception of reality. Ensure the victory of Donald in the election of the US President. Then create a political alliance between the United States, France, Russia (and a number of other states) and establish a new world order.

Our idea was insane, but realizable.

In order to understand everything for the beginning, it was necessary to "digitize" all possible types of modern man.

Donald decided to invite for this task—the special scientific department of the "Cambridge University."

British scientists from Cambridge Analytica suggested making 5,000 existing human psychotypes—the "ideal image" of a possible Trump supporter. Then .. put this image back on all psychotypes and thus pick up a universal key to anyone and everyone.

Then it was only necessary to upload this data to information flows and social networks. And we began to look for those who would have coped with this task better than others.

At the very beginning of the brave and romantic [story] was not very much. A pair of hacker groups, civil journalists from WikiLeaks and political strategist Mikhail Kovalev.

The next step was to develop a system for transferring tasks and information, so that no intelligence and NSA could burn it.

Though the posts don't directly confirm collusion with the Trump campaign, Rykov's use of "we" and "our" strongly suggests some level of coordination. Short of accessing his Direct Messages, the claim that Trump sent Rykov a private message on election night 2012 is unverifiable.

The picture that Rykov included, however, was not an original picture. Analyzing the source code on the Instagram photo confirms that Rykov posted the picture of Trump approximately six hours after Melania Trump posted it on her Twitter: the code included "taken_at_timestamp": 1352268891". Running a time conversion from that Unix timestamp shows the official time as Tuesday, 6 November 2012 at 22:14:51.

Though this was not an original image, it is not out of the realm of possibility that Trump sent DMs of the picture to those who were praising him on Twitter. The mention of working with WikiLeaks is especially interesting, given the fact that President Trump's CIA Director Mike Pompeo has said that WikiLeaks is a "hostile intelligence service" acting as an arm of the Kremlin. A year after the election, it was revealed that Donald Trump Jr. was in contact with WikiLeaks and aided the organization in spreading the contents of the Russian hacking efforts.

Throughout 2015 and 2016, Rykov was a vocal supporter of Donald Trump. He set up a website dedicated to aggregating and promoting positive news on Trump, and was featured in the conservative *Washington Examiner* in a piece titled "Putin Loves Donald Trump" as a "Kremlin mouthpiece."

Then-candidate Trump retweeted the article.

Establishing Rykov's proximity to the Kremlin

Konstantin Rykov has a long and complicated history in Russian politics and popular culture. In the late 1990s and early 2000s, Rykov was somewhat of an online pioneer creating multiple websites focused on culture, news, and politics. In 2007, as a twenty-eight-year-old, Rykov was elected to the Duma as a deputy in Vladimir Putin's United Russia party. The tech-savvy Rykov quickly became one of Russia's most influential politicians. He has remained an ardent supporter of Putin, creating numerous websites dedicated to the Russian President. In *The Net Delusion: The Dark Side of Internet Freedom*, renowned political/tech scientist Evgeny Morozov explained that, "Russian leaders follow [Rykov's] lead."

Rykov's far-right vision is world-wide. He has supported the Scottish

Independence effort in 2014, Brexit in the UK, Marine Le Pen in France and Donald Trump in the United States. The Kremlin propagandist's influential position in the Kremlin was further established in 2015 when hacked text messages were released by Anonymous International that show continual discussion between Rykov and Putin adviser Timur Prokopenko—the head of the Russian domestic affairs department.

The two men discuss a *quid pro quo* between French far-right leader Marine Le Pen and the Kremlin. Le Pen was to recognize the Russian annexation of Crimea as legitimate in exchange for Russian money in the form of large loans. Le Pen denies knowing Rykov or Prokopenko and maintains her innocence, despite the fact that she did recognize Crimea and then subsequently received over forty million euros in loans from Moscow's First Czech-Russian Bank. The cash-strapped National Front Party was previously denied loans from French banks.

Further eroding the credibility of Le Pen, an investigative report by the French newspaper *Navalny* revealed that Rykov owns a $2 million villa in the town of Mougins. He is listed as a tax resident of France, meaning that he must either permanently live in France, work there, or have his main economic interests in France. Rykov claims he lives in Moscow. He did not return requests for comment.

Rykov's shared associates with Trump

Rykov is one degree of separation away from Trump in two different areas. First, recall that during Trump's trip to Moscow in 2013, he was seen with Yulya Alferova nearly every step of the way. She even claimed that Trump was running for President in January of 2015, months before he would announce his run. Alferova's husband is tech entrepreneur Artem Klyushin, who regularly corresponds with Rykov on social media. He was with Alferova and Trump throughout Trump's time in Moscow. In March of 2016, Klyushin posted pictures with Rykov in what he called a "secret meeting." The exact topic of the meeting remains unknown.

Second, former Fox News producer Jack Hanick was a special guest at a Trump election night party in Moscow organized by Rykov.

Hanick co-founded a conservative Orthodox TV channel in Russia called Tsargrad TV with Putin's close confidant Konstantin Malofeev. Tsargrad was the only major channel to cover Carter Page's full speech in Moscow in 2015, the pro-Trump parties on election night, and the Inauguration. Hanick has regularly appeared on his channel, defending the alt-right and denouncing "globalists." A former associate of Hanick's, who demanded anonymity, told me that Hanick still occasionally keeps in contact with his Fox News friends.

A regular commentator on Tsargrad is former Russian intelligence officer Leonid Reshetnikov. He is also the former head of the think tank Russian Institute for Strategic Studies (RISS). In April, *Reuters* reported that Reshetnikov's RISS was the group responsible for drawing up the plan for the 2016 US election interference campaign.

The revelations about Konstantin Rykov, his confession of working with WikiLeaks and hacker groups, and his shared associations with the Kremlin and Donald Trump are troubling. He is yet another figure in an ever-expanding investigation into possible collusion between the Trump campaign and the Russian government.

February 26, 2018
Kremlin Propagandist Who Claimed He Coordinated with Trump Team was Previously Appointed as Putin's "Trusted Confidant"

Konstantin Rykov boasted about his four year plan to "free America and make it great again."

- In his November 2016 Facebook post, Rykov said he worked with a team of hacker groups and Wikileaks.
- New evidence paints a picture of Rykov not as a Putin-supporting blogger but a plausibly deniable asset for the Kremlin.
- During the 2012 election, Vladimir Putin appointed Rykov as a "trusted confidant," granting him access to the President and indicating a level of trust by Russian government.

The Kremlin propagandist who boasted on his Facebook page that he worked with Trump, WikiLeaks, and a team of hackers to influence the 2016 US election was appointed in 2012 as one of Putin's "trusted confidants." Konstantin Rykov was personally summoned by Putin's election campaign chief Stanislav Govorukhin to serve in this role as a trusted representative of the Putin campaign.

Days after the 2016 US election, Rykov posted on Facebook a detailed story of how he received a Direct Message from Trump in 2012, the beginning of a four-year plan to elect Trump to the Presidency.

> It's time for wonderful stories. I'll tell you about (now it's possible) how Donald Trump and I decided to free America and make it great again. This took us as much as 4 years and 2 more days. . . .
>
> At the beginning of the brave and romantic [story] was not very much. A pair of hacker groups, civil journalists from WikiLeaks and political strategist Mikhail Kovalev.
>
> The next step was to develop a system for transferring tasks and information, so that no intelligence and NSA could burn it.

Since the moment Trump announced his candidacy, Rykov was an ardent public supporter. In the *Washington Post*, Rykov was described as a "Putin supporter"; in the *Atlantic* he's portrayed as a "pro-Kremlin blogger." A fuller picture paints a different story of Rykov—an asset utilized by the Kremlin to do its dirty work with a level of deniability.

In order to drum up support and promote his message, Putin created an institution of trusted representatives—in Russian, "trusted faces"—according to Ilya Zaslavskiy, the Head of Research at the Free Russia Foundation, a US non-profit. Zaslavskiy said that the group of trusted confidants usually consists of around five hundred "cultural figures and celebrities who meet [Putin] and get televised as his supporters." These representatives are trusted by Putin himself and are often rewarded with "various small and not so small privileges after elections," according to Zaslavskiy.

Personally appointed by Putin's election chief, Rykov was one of the most important members of the 2012 group of trusted confidants. His boisterous, unwavering support of Putin was broadcast daily to his hundreds of thousands of social media followers.

The revelation about Rykov's proximity to Putin during the 2012 election is the starkest example of the internet guru's significance to the Russian government. From the mid-2000s through 2014, there are multiple instances of Rykov interacting with and on behalf of the Kremlin.

In 2007, the *Washington Post* identified Rykov as a blogger from whom the Russian government took direction on internet-issues. "The pearl of Rykov's media empire is the two-year-old *Vzglyad* ("View") online newspaper," the *Post* wrote, "which features a serious-looking news section with stories toeing the Kremlin line and a lifestyle section that covers the latest in luxury cars and interior design. Surveys rank *Vzglyad* as one of Russia's five most-visited news sites."

Anton Nossik, a Russian journalist who wrote about corruption in Putin's Russia, said that Vladislav Surkov—Putin's personal political adviser—organized private funding for Rykov. Nossik died suddenly in 2017 of an alleged heart attack.

In 2009, Rykov was "rewarded" with a position in the Russian government at the State Duma. Two years later, as Rykov was preparing to leave his position at the Duma, renowned political/tech scientist Evgeny Morozov explained that "Russian leaders follow [Rykov's] lead." Morozov went on to write that Rykov shaped the Kremlin's online propaganda machine.

During Marine Le Pen's rise in France in 2014, the Kremlin again relied on Rykov to negotiate on behalf of the Russian government. Leaked text messages revealed that influential Kremlin adviser Timur Prokopenko was in communication with Rykov, who supposedly had access to Le Pen. The messages detail an alleged *quid pro quo* wherein Le Pen would recognize the annexation of Crimea in exchange for financial support from Russia.

"She hasn't betrayed our expectations," the Kremlin official replied.

"It will be necessary to thank the French in one way or another.... It's important," [Rykov] said.

"Yes. Super!" the Kremlin official responded.

Le Pen publicly recognized Crimea as part of Russian territory and subsequently received over forty million euros in Russian-backed loans to her Front National party. She denies that the two events are related.

This series of events portrays Rykov not as simply a pro-Kremlin blogger, but instead as a strategic asset working for Putin. For the better part of a decade, Rykov has allegedly received funding from senior Russian government officials and acted with their blessing.

Former senior US officials who I knew had knowledge of Rykov were not interested in discussing him. Rykov did not immediately return requests for comment.

Russian experts with whom I've spoken put varying levels of credibility behind Rykov's claims of working with Trump; none were particularly convinced. There was more of a consensus in the plausibility of Rykov being part of the information warfare campaign that Russia launched against the 2016 US election.

Nearly all, though, agreed that Rykov's claims were not frivolous or without meaning. Whether accurate or not, Vladimir Putin wanted the United States population to see these claims.

A spokesman for special counsel Robert Mueller declined to comment on Rykov. Mueller continues to investigate if the Trump campaign coordinated with the Russian government in their US election interference campaign.

Subsequent Information

In August 2018, Mr. Manafort was convicted in Virginia on eight counts of tax fraud, bank fraud, and hiding foreign bank accounts. Under federal sentencing guidelines, Mr. Manafort faced roughly seven to ten years in prison on the tax counts alone. His conviction on money laundering and foreign agent charges was to be handled in Washington, DC, separate from the charges in Virginia.

After resisting the government's efforts to get him to plead guilty and cooperate for over a year in Washington DC, Mr. Manafort eventually agreed with their requests, and, in September 2018, he pleaded guilty to one count of conspiracy against the US and one count of conspiracy to obstruct justice.

The obstruction charge by using intimidation or force against a witness, and also with tampering with a witness, was also levied against Mr. Kilimnik. The superseding indictment filed by Mr. Mueller alleged that Mr. Manafort and Mr. Kilimnik conspired to influence witness testimony in the upcoming trials. Mr. Kilimnik resides in Russia and thus was not arraigned.

Two months after Mr. Manafort finally agreed to plead guilty and cooperate with Mr. Mueller's probe into Russian interference, the plea deal fell apart as Mr. Mueller reported that Mr. Manafort continued to lie to the FBI and other investigators.

"After signing the plea agreement, Manafort committed federal crimes by lying to the Federal Bureau of Investigation and the Special Counsel's Office on a variety of subject matters, which constitute breaches of the agreement," Mr. Mueller said. Both sides agreed that the judge should move forward with sentencing, which, combined with his convictions in Virginia, will likely keep Mr. Manafort in prison for the rest of his life.

Mr. Manafort's full involvement with Russians during the 2016 election, including his communications with Mr. Deripaska via Mr. Kilimnik, have yet to be brought to light.

Questions about Carter Page's involvement in the Russia investigation lingered more than two years after Mr. Steele wrote his reports on the alleged significant role that Mr. Page played in the Trump-Russia conspiracy. Mr. Mueller's prosecutors didn't seem to be interviewing witnesses close to Mr. Page or Mr. Page himself, which could be a sign that either Mr. Page was a target of the investigation or that investigators had disproven some of the claims made against him. Given the FISA warrant issued and renewed four times on Mr. Page, the government likely already had the information necessary to map out his activities in 2016 and 2017.

Cambridge Analytica and its parent company SCL Group filed for insolvency proceedings and closed operations as of May 2018. Mr. Mueller requested and received all emails and communications of Cambridge Analytica's executives to ascertain the level of Russian involvement.

Finally, Mr. Rykov largely escaped scrutiny as mainstream media refused to report on his suspicious and intriguing social media posts.

Former United States Ambassador to Russia Michael McFaul briefly weighed in on the story in September 2017, however, writing, "Rykov works for the Kremlin. (let's not be naive about these things)."

Abstract

Mr. Trump's campaign was dogged by a relentless amount of suspicious activity: money transfers, overnight flights, shady business dealings involving those associated with the campaign, and a Kremlin propagandist taking credit for the surprise election results. Some of this activity seemed to corroborate or at least lend credence to Mr. Steele's dossier, which reached the conclusion that there was a vast conspiracy between the Trump campaign and the Russian government.

The cast of characters with whom Mr. Trump chose to surround himself conducted activity that raised more than a few red flags. The dubious activity of Mr. Manafort, Mr. Page, Cambridge Analytica, and others during the 2016 campaign has, if nothing else, left a mountain of evidence for Mr. Mueller to investigate. Whether he reaches the same conclusion that Mr. Steele reached in the summer of 2016 remains to be seen.

Epilogue

M
R. MUELLER'S INVESTIGATION RACKED UP DOZENS of criminal charges against the Russians who meddled in the 2016 election as well as the inner circle of Mr. Trump's campaign. As it neared the two-year mark, the investigators, speaking only through court documents and proceedings, began to paint a picture of a presidential campaign willing to engage with operatives from the hostile country that interfered in our election. The walls slowly closed around the historically unpopular President, and with each indictment and guilty plea, his fate darkened.

The conclusion of the Mueller probe won't signal the end of the legal trouble for President Trump, but rather offer a roadmap for possible impeachment. Investigating every aspect of Mr. Trump's campaign and its various misdeeds would take many years, political capital that Mr. Mueller does not have in this hyperpartisan era. Sections of the broader Russia investigation will undoubtedly move forward after Mr. Mueller's role has ended, as officials at the DOJ continue to hold those who broke federal law accountable for their actions.

Events that occurred within the Trump campaign in 2015 and 2016 continue to be revealed on a weekly basis, more than two years after Mr. Trump's shocking victory. The Russia investigation is an ongoing, ever-changing monster that will take years to fully uncover, and even longer to analyze and understand the full implications—even without new dis- and misinformation being spread constantly online.

In late 2018, I was among a handful of journalists who received an unsolicited email from a person who purported to be a former co-worker of Robert Mueller who was being offered money by a GOP provocateur to make up sexual harassment claims against Mr. Mueller. Unable to confirm any of the details, and not wanting to draw any attention to a possible "plant" of a fake news story to discredit journalists, my cohorts and I refused to write anything about this email.

Weeks passed and the woman who originally sent the email refused to speak on the phone, provide any documentation, or confirm any of her story with evidence. I was fairly certain that this was a dirty trick to paint journalists as providers of fake news. However, in late October, Jacob Wohl, whose Wikipedia page describes him as a "far-right scammer, conspiracy theorist, online blogger, Internet troll," tweeted that he had sources telling him that a scandalous story about Mr. Mueller was about to break:

> Several media sources tell me that a scandalous story about Mueller is breaking tomorrow. Should be interesting. Stay tuned!

News quickly spread that sexual assault claims were going to be levied against Mr. Mueller. It was now clear that this was at least somewhat of a legitimate GOP effort to attack Mr. Mueller. I felt an intense duty to sound the alarm.

"I wasn't going to report on this, but I think my fears are coming true", I tweeted. "Based on information that I am privy to, I believe false accusations will be spread about Mueller in order to discredit him and possibly the journalists who are preparing this story."

The following day, Mr. Wohl and GOP lobbyist Jack Burkman announced their intentions to bring forward at least one woman who apparently was willing to make up claims about Mr. Mueller. The woman never publicly came forward, and the "intelligence company" that was allegedly gathering the information turned out to be an embarrassingly amateurish attempt by Mr. Wohl to make the operation look legitimate. The phone number registered to Surefire Intelligence's website connected to Mr. Wohl's mother, for example.

With their scheme outed, the story faded and the effort to smear Mr. Mueller was debunked before it could begin. Mr. Mueller's office referred the matter to the FBI and they opened an investigation into the actions of Mr. Wohl, Mr. Burkman, and others.

The episode remains a stark example of the depths to which some are willing to sink to discredit, tarnish, and delegitimize Mr. Mueller—a decorated war hero and lifelong public servant.

For journalists like myself, the work to protect the crucial Mueller investigation and bring the facts of the 2016 election to the public endures. I continue to talk to sources, dig through documents, and conduct open-source research. These efforts increasingly are bearing fruit.

I find hope in journalists, researchers, and public figures who believe truth still exists in the political world. To that end, I want to conclude this part of my journey with a list of people who I regularly find to be beacons of sanity in this otherwise crazy time. If you read the work and analysis of these professionals, you will not only be better informed about the Russia investigation, but your sense of optimism for the future of truth will surge.

In no particular order:

George Conway
Natasha Bertrand
Preet Bharara
Ronan Farrow
Jane Mayer
Carole Cadwalladr
Evan McMullin
Caroline Orr
Jason Leopold
Anthony Cormier
Joyce Vance
Michael Steele
Jonathan Landay

Who's Who:
A Glossary of Key Trump-Russia Figures

Aras Agalarov: Azerbaijani-Russian billionaire close to President Putin.

Emin Agalarov: Son of Aras Agalarov. Close friend of the Trump family since 2013.

Yulia Alferova: Employee of Aras Agalarov's business empire who helped organize Miss Universe 2013.

John Bolton: Former Ambassador to the UN under George Bush, current Trump National Security Adviser.

Maria Butina: Young Russian assistant to Mr. Torshin

Cambridge Analytica: Data analysis company hired by Mr. Cruz, Mr. Carson and then Mr. Trump.

Michael Cohen: Mr. Trump's longtime lawyer and "fixer." Vice President of the Trump Organization.

Oleg Deripaska: One of Russia's most powerful billionaires, on whom Mr. Putin regularly relies.

Paul Erickson: Republican operative who advised many GOP campaigns.

Ike Kaveladze: The Agalarov's Vice President and right-hand businessman.

David Keene: Former President of the NRA.

Konstantin Kilimnik: Russian intelligence-trained political adviser and strategist.

Jared Kushner: Son-in-law of Donald Trump. Acted as one of the lead decision-makers in Mr. Trump's campaign.

Paul Manafort: Mr. Trump's longtime friend and Campaign Chairman in the Summer of 2016.

Joseph Mifsud: Maltese professor who is well-connected to Russian government officials.

Sergei Millian: Belarusian-American businessman who previously worked alongside Mr. Trump.

George Nader: Lebanese-American businessman and lobbyist with strong relationships with Middle East leaders.

Carter Page: Former Trump campaign foreign policy adviser.

George Papadopoulos: Former Trump campaign foreign policy adviser.

Simona Mangiante Papadopoulos: Wife of Mr. Papadopoulos, who also worked for Mr. Mifsud in 2016, before meeting her soon-to-be husband.

Samuel Patten: Republican political consultant and lobbyist who contracted with Cambridge Analytica.

Erik Prince: Informal Trump campaign adviser with longstanding Republican connections. Sister Betsy DeVos became Mr. Trump's Secretary of Education.

Andrey Rozov: Moscow based real estate developer who has been associated with Mr. Sater for nearly a decade.

Konstantin Rykov: Russian government internet pioneer, propagandist and former politician.

Felix Sater: Russian mob-connected real estate developer and former assistant to Mr. Trump. Cooperated and provided valuable information to the FBI in counter-terrorism cases.

Alexander Torshin: Mafia-connected Russian politician and banker.

Donald Trump Jr.: Son of Donald Trump. Close political adviser in 2015 and 2016 Executive Vice President of the Trump Organization.

Natalia Veselnitskaya: Russian attorney connected to military intelligence and top Kremlin officials.

Julian Wheatland: Cambridge Analytica executive.

Joel Zamel: Australian-Israeli social media expert and political scientist.

Personal Acknowledgments

I have to start by thanking my family. I won the lottery in life by being born into a family that not only supports my decisions but privately and publicly roots for my success. I owe all of my professional accomplishments to the safety and comfort of knowing that my family will be there for me. Mom, Dad, Sammy, Joey, Mimi, Megan, David, Topher, Jordan, I am eternally grateful for you.

To Nate, Josh, and the rest of the group chat boys, thank you for keeping me sane and grounded. Your friendship means the world to me.

To Jane and Maggie, you have been there through all of my ups and downs and still love me for who I am. How did I get so lucky? Thank you for always supporting my decisions, big and small.

To Olivia, DJ, Dani, Kaitlyn, welcoming me into your lives at a time in my life when I felt uncertain about almost everything meant more to me than I can express. Knowing that you like me for me adds a comfort level to my life that makes being with you feel like home. I love spending time with you guys. Here's to many more years of shenanigans.

To George, Eryn, Evelyn, Gregg, Benny, Noa, Maddy, Kenzo, Jackee, Natali, Lauren, Matthieu, Eric, and everyone else who have played such an important role in my life, individually and collectively, over the years, thank you.

Scott Stedman is an investigative journalist active in covering the Trump-Russia scandal. He has written articles for the *Guardian* and the *Atlantic* and has been cited in, among others, the *Washington Post*, BBC, *Reuters*, CNN, *McClatchy*, *Vox*, and *VICE*. He studied Political Science with an emphasis on American government at the University of California, Irvine, and received his bachelor's degree in 2018.